12/95

American Events

THE ASSASSINATION OF PRESIDENT JOHN F. KENNEDY

Patricia D. Netzley

New Discovery Books
New York

Maxwell Macmillan Canada
Toronto

Maxwell Macmillan International
New York Oxford Singapore Sydney

Book design: Deborah Fillion
Cover photo courtesy of Brown Brothers

New Discovery Books
Macmillan Publishing Company
866 Third Avenue
New York, NY 10022

Maxwell Macmillan Canada, Inc.
1200 Eglinton Avenue East
Suite 200
Don Mills, Ontario M3C 3N1

Macmillan Publishing Company is part of the Maxwell Communication
Group of Companies.

First Edition

Printed in the United States of America

10 9 8 7 6 5 4 3 2 1

Library of Congress Cataloging-in-Publication Data

Netzley, Patricia D.
     The assassination of President John F. Kennedy / by Patricia D.
Netzley. — 1st ed.
          p. cm. — (American Events)
     Includes bibliographical references and index.
     ISBN 0-02-768127-0
     1. Kennedy, John F. (John Fitzgerald), 1917–1963—Assassination—
Juvenile literature. [1. Kennedy, John F. (John Fitzgerald), 1917–1963—
Assassination.] I. Title. II. Series.
     E842.9.N42 1993
     973.922—dc20   93-20818
     Summary: An examination of the events leading up to and coming after the
assassination of President John F. Kennedy, including the assassination of Lee
Harvey Oswald and the convening of the Warren Commission.

The author wishes to thank Ray for his encouragement;

Matthew, Sarah, and Jacob for their patience;

and the Faber grandparents for all of that baby-sitting.

Mourners at the funeral for President John F. Kennedy look on as representatives from the four branches of the armed forces fold the American flag that was draped over the coffin.

CONTENTS

The Kennedy motorcade in Dallas, November 22, 1963, en route from Love Field to the Trade Mart

Chapter 1

THE ROAD TO DALLAS

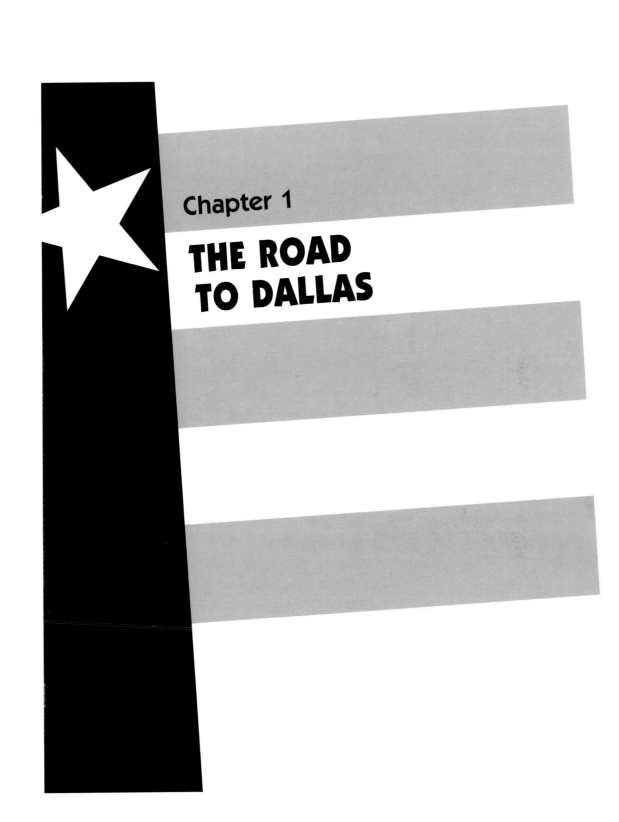

J ohn Fitzgerald Kennedy did not always want to become president of the United States. As a boy, he thought he might someday be a lawyer or a writer, natural choices for a person in poor health who spent a lot of time reading. But his parents had something else in mind for him. They wanted him to follow family tradition and go into politics.

John's grandfather Patrick Joseph Kennedy had served three terms in the Massachusetts senate, and his father, Joseph (Joe) Kennedy, had been appointed ambassador to Great Britain by President Franklin D. Roosevelt. John's mother, Rose Fitzgerald Kennedy, also loved politics. Her father, John F. Fitzgerald, had been the first Catholic ever elected to the House of Representatives, and he had spent six years as the mayor of Boston. He took Rose to the White House to meet President William McKinley when she was in high school, and McKinley made the Fitzgerald family feel a part of his campaigns.

Together, Joe and Rose Kennedy decided that they wanted at least one of their four sons to enter politics. They had money and power, and they told all nine of their children that the only thing that mattered in life was being the best at everything. "We want winners. We don't want losers here," said Joe.[1] They pushed John, whom the family also called Jack, into

John F. Kennedy (seated on bike) with (from left to right) his mother, Rose; Eunice;
Kathleen; Rosemary; and Joe, Jr.

competing against his brothers and sisters in various sports, even though Jack had a weak back. Jack tried very hard to win the swimming and boating races, but he usually lost to his older brother, Joe Jr.

Joe Jr. was the family favorite. Strong and intelligent, he was the one their father decided would eventually be president. Joe Jr. went to the best schools and had special privileges at home. "Joe [Jr.] was clearly the kind of man his father would have liked to have been," said a friend.[2] Soon Jack began to feel second best. No matter what he tried, it seemed that his brother always outdid him. Joe Jr. was better at sports, better in school, and better at receiving his father's praise.

Not until he was in college did Jack find a way to surpass his older brother's successes. As a part of his studies in political science, he wrote a book, *Why England Slept*, about Britain's readiness for World War II, which had just begun in Europe. The book was published in 1940 and immediately became a best-seller. It made Jack Kennedy a celebrity, and more important to him than that, it made his father proud of him.

The following year Jack enlisted in the navy and was given a desk job with naval intelligence in Washington, D.C. But this wasn't exciting enough for him, so he volunteered for duty on a patrol torpedo (PT) boat and completed his PT training, hoping to be sent where the fighting was going on. To his disappointment, the navy assigned him to be an instructor at the naval base. Jack called his father and asked for his help in getting a transfer. The next day Jack was given command of PT-109 in the South Pacific. "I worked hard at it because I liked PTs," Jack later said. "I think I liked PTs because they were small."[3]

PT boats were also difficult to pilot. "They had no radio, they had no radar, they had no lights," explained Kennedy friend Robert Donovan, who wrote a book about PT-109. "Everyone knew they were a joke."[4] One night, during a mission in the Blackett Strait between two of the Solomon Islands, a Japanese destroyer rammed PT-109. Two men were killed, and Kennedy convinced the remaining ten to swim for land. "I know I'm the skipper of this PT crew and I can still give you orders," he told his crew. "But most of you men are older than I am. I have nothing to lose, but some of you

JFK on board PT-109 in the Samoa Islands in 1943

have wives and children, and I'm not going to order you to try to swim to that shore. You'll have to make your own decision on that."[5]

Everyone decided to follow him. Some clung to a board as they swam, while Kennedy, despite a bad back, towed an injured crewman behind him by holding a strap from the man's life jacket in his teeth. It took them four hours to reach a deserted atoll. Once his men were safely on land, Kennedy went back into the ocean to look for help. He soon discovered there were no other U.S. ships nearby, and he returned to his men discouraged and exhausted. Two days later he decided to lead his men on another swim. They reached a nearby island after three hours in the water but found it to be deserted, too. The next day Kennedy and another man continued on alone to still another island, where they eventually found two local inhabitants who agreed to take a message to U.S. authorities for them. The crew of PT-109 was rescued.

In June 1944 Kennedy went to the New England Baptist Hospital in Boston to undergo surgery on his back, which had been hurt during his ordeal. While he was at the hospital, he was awarded the Navy and Marine Corps medal for bravery. The *New Yorker* magazine published an article about the PT-109 incident, "Survival" by John Hersey, which was later reprinted in *Reader's Digest*, and the 26-year-old Kennedy became one of America's most famous heroes.

Kennedy's happiness at his fame was short-lived. Joe Jr., jealous over the attention his younger brother was receiving, volunteered to fly a dangerous bombing mission. He hoped to become a hero, too, but his plane exploded and he was killed. Jack was grief-stricken. He put together a book entitled *As We Remember Joe*, which was privately published in 1945, the year the war ended. Of his older brother, Jack said, "I seriously think that of all the people I have ever met Joe had truly the mark of greatness in him."[6]

Now Jack's father began telling him that he should run for public office in his brother's place. "My father wanted his eldest son in politics," Jack once explained. "'Wanted' isn't the right word. He *demanded* it."[7] Jack decided to follow his father's wishes. In 1946 he won the first race he entered, becoming a congressman from the 11th district in Boston. Later, despite increasingly poor health, he was reelected for a second and then a third term.

In 1952 Kennedy decided to run for the U.S. Senate. Just before announcing his candidacy, he traveled with his brother Robert (Bobby) to the Far East. One of the countries he visited was Vietnam, whose people were fighting to end more than 70 years of French rule. The effects of this war on the Vietnamese were terrible; many lived in poverty. When Kennedy returned to the United States and began his Senate campaign, he made speeches in favor of Vietnam's independence from the French.

Kennedy's opponent for the Senate seat was a well-respected Republican named Henry Cabot Lodge. Because Lodge was older and more experienced, Kennedy was not expected to win. Lodge himself boasted, "I'm going to win by 300,000 votes."[8] Then the entire Kennedy family went to work on the campaign, traveling all across Massachusetts to gain support. Rose held 33 tea parties for her son, and she appeared on a television program entitled "Coffee with the Kennedys." Kennedy's sisters went door-to-door canvassing votes for him, and his brother Bobby sometimes gave speeches in his place. At one of these, he spoke only a moment, saying, "My brother Jack couldn't be here, my mother couldn't be here, my sister Eunice couldn't be here, my sister Pat couldn't be here, my sister Jean couldn't be here, but if my brother Jack were here, he'd tell you Lodge has a very bad voting record. Thank you."[9]

But no one was more active in his campaign than Jack himself. He visited 351 cities and towns, attending meetings, giving speeches, and making public appearances. He also participated in two debates against Lodge, during which he impressed audiences with his quick thinking, broad knowledge, and easy confidence. In the end his rigorous campaigning paid off. He received 51.5 percent of the vote, winning by a margin of more than 70,000 votes.

Also elected that fall was President Dwight D. Eisenhower. In January 1953 Kennedy attended his inaugural ball. His date for the event was Jacqueline Bouvier, the daughter of a wealthy and socially prominent family. Jackie was elegant, refined, and well schooled in several foreign languages, and the two made an attractive couple. They were married on September 12, 1953.

A little over a year after the wedding, Kennedy decided to undergo another operation on his back. He had been experiencing a great deal of pain and could barely walk, even on crutches. Unfortunately, the surgery wasn't successful. Kennedy almost died from an infection, and it was months before he recovered. From then on he had to wear a special brace to support his spine.

Kennedy spent his convalescence writing a book entitled *Profiles in Courage*. He wanted to tell "the stories of the pressures experienced by eight United States Senators and the grace with which they endured them—the risks to their careers, the unpopularity of their courses, the defamation of their characters, and sometimes, but sadly only sometimes, the vindication of their reputations and their principles."[10] The book immediately became a best-seller and later won the Pulitzer Prize, the foremost U.S. literary award.

Kennedy was very proud of *Profiles in Courage*. He also hoped its publication would help his chances to become the Democrats' candidate for vice president during the 1956 election. But during the Democratic National Convention, someone else was chosen instead. Kennedy gave a speech praising the nominee, Estes Kefauver, and so impressed the public with his graciousness that when he ran for reelection to the Senate in 1958, he won by a huge margin. This success eventually led to his selection over Lyndon B. Johnson, a powerful Texas senator, as the 1960 Democratic candidate for president. Kennedy then chose Johnson as his vice presidential running mate.

Kennedy's Republican opponent in the election was Richard M. Nixon, the current vice president. Nixon had an advantage coming into the race, because President Eisenhower and his administration were so popular. Kennedy was also hurt by his youth and his religion. At 43, he would be the youngest man ever to be elected president, and he was Catholic, which made people worry that he would be heavily influenced by the pope.

Kennedy worked hard to overcome these concerns. He campaigned

Kennedy campaigns in West Virginia during the 1960 presidential election.

relentlessly, and his friendly, easygoing style made him a success with voters. He reminded people often of his war record, and his supporters wore special buttons or tiepins that were shaped like PT boats and said "Kennedy in '60." He also participated in a series of televised debates, during which he looked calm and confident beside Nixon, who appeared tired and pale. "There can be no question but that Kennedy had gained more from the debates than I," Nixon later admitted.[11]

Still, the Democrat's lead was slim. Said one pollster, "It can go either way. This has been the most volatile campaign since we began taking samplings in 1936. I have never seen the lead change hands so many times."[12] When the election was finally held, Kennedy won by the slimmest margin in history. He took 49.7 percent of the vote; Nixon, 49.6.

On January 20, 1961, John Fitzgerald Kennedy was inaugurated the 35th president of the United States. He immediately set out to win the full support of the American public. He invited reporters to interview and photograph him and his family, which by this time included two children, Caroline and John F., Jr., nicknamed John-John. These were the first children to live in the White House since Teddy Roosevelt's in the early 1900s, and they were a popular subject for many newspaper and magazine articles.

The president also appeared frequently on television. He was the first elected official to hold live, televised press conferences, and the audience for his first conference on January 25, 1961, was more than 60 million people. In all he would hold 62 more televised conferences. Perhaps the most difficult of these occurred when he had to explain his involvement in the Bay of Pigs disaster.

The Bay of Pigs lies off the southwest coast of Cuba, a Communist country ruled by Fidel Castro. When Kennedy became president, he learned that an agency of the U.S. government, the Central Intelligence Agency (CIA), had secretly been training Cuban exiles so that they could invade Cuba and overthrow Castro. Kennedy reluctantly allowed the training sessions to continue.

The exiles' plan was to sail to Cuba and land men on its beaches once

John F. Kennedy is inaugurated as the 35th president of the United States.

a group of B-26 bombers had destroyed Castro's air force. The bombers struck on April 15, 1961, but they failed to damage three of Cuba's powerful T-33 fighter jets. The CIA asked the president to authorize another air strike two days later to eliminate these jets. Kennedy agreed; however, someone from the White House, apparently acting on the president's orders, called off the mission just before the bombers were scheduled to take off.

Consequently, when the exiles landed on Cuban beaches, Castro's jets were there and proceeded to spray them with gunfire, sink their ships, and shoot down 16 of their B-26s. Castro's forces either captured or killed all of the invaders, and the U.S. government was unable to hide its involvement in the plan any longer.

Kennedy took full blame for the Bay of Pigs incident. "I'm the president," he said. "I could have decided otherwise. It's my responsibility."[13] Yet later he fired many of the members of the CIA responsible for the plan. In September 1961 he announced that John McCone would replace Allen Dulles as the head of the CIA.

One and a half years after the Bay of Pigs disaster, another crisis erupted in Cuba: Soviet Premier Nikita Khrushchev began shipping intermediate-range nuclear missiles to Castro. President Kennedy sent 63 ships, some from neighboring Latin America, out to form a blockade, announcing that "all ships of any kind bound for Cuba from whatever nation or port will, if found to contain cargoes of offensive weapons, be turned back."[14] He added that if any of the Cuban missiles were ever fired, the U.S. would launch "a fully retaliatory response upon the Soviet Union."[15]

Khrushchev threatened to sink any ships that interfered with his own. He ordered his vessels to continue to Cuba, but in the end, when they reached the blockade, he decided to call them back. Khrushchev then said he would withdraw all missiles already in Cuba if Kennedy would promise never to invade that country again. After the president signed a letter agreeing to leave Cuba alone, the Soviets removed their missiles.

The media praised Kennedy for the way he had handled the crisis. One columnist wrote, "President Kennedy has interpreted correctly the wishes of the American people. The nation has demanded that the United States protest vigorously the Soviet invasion of Cuba and use force if necessary to assure the safety of the countries of this hemisphere."[16] But Cubans living in America, who still wanted to see Castro overthrown, criticized the president for his actions.

Certain conservative groups also spoke out against Kennedy, accusing him of being too "soft" on Communists. They felt the country should keep making nuclear weapons and preparing itself for war. President Kennedy did not agree with this. He said, "If you could think *only* of yourself, it would be easy to say you'd press the button [to launch a nuclear attack], and easy to press it, too. It may sound corny but I am not thinking so much of our world, but the world that [my daughter] Caroline will live in."[17] According to David Ormsby-Gore, the British ambassador during that time, President Kennedy saw the issue "in terms of children—his children and everybody else's children. And then that's where his passion came in, that's when his emotion came in."[18]

The president began speaking out about the need for peace between the United States and the Soviet Union. He also told several people he wanted to "get the Americans out of Vietnam."[19] According to one reporter, the president "seemed sick of [the war] and frequently asked how to be rid of the commitment."[20] "It [is] their country and their responsibility and their war," he told his secretary of defense.[21] Such statements angered many U.S. military leaders.

Another target for criticism was Kennedy's involvement in the civil rights movement. During the early 1960s, African-Americans still did not have equal rights under the law, and in many parts of the country, particularly the South, people did not want this to change. Governor George Wallace of Alabama, among others, challenged the president's efforts to enforce laws that ended segregation, saying, "From this cradle of the Confederacy, this very heart of the great Anglo-Saxon Southland . . . I draw the line in the dust and toss the gauntlet before the feet of tyranny. And I say, Segregation now! Segregation tomorrow! Segregation forever!"[22]

THE ASSASSINATION OF PRESIDENT JOHN F. KENNEDY

Kennedy had other enemies besides the segregationists. Members of the Mafia, a crime organization, hated both him and his brother Robert, whom the president had appointed attorney general. Robert Kennedy was determined to stamp out all organized crime in America. "If we do not on a national scale attack organized criminals . . . they will destroy us," he said.[23] The Mafia felt this was a betrayal, because they had once worked secretly with the government in a plot to assassinate Castro. Crime bosses like Carlos Marcello threatened to kill the president.

President Kennedy's advisers were worried about his safety. The president himself often commented on how easy it would be for someone to kill him while he was giving a speech or greeting the crowds. According to biographer Ralph Martin, "Kennedy talked a great deal about death, and about the assassination of Lincoln."[24] Yet the president could not hide in the White House. "If someone is going to kill me, they're going to kill me," Kennedy said.[25] He refused to worry about the dangers of being out in public, and he began planning a trip to announce his bid for reelection in 1964.

Kennedy chose Texas as the place to start his campaign. He had been losing popularity there, and he needed to strengthen his chances of winning in the southern states. He asked his wife, Jackie, to accompany him because he knew the voters liked her, and she agreed to introduce the president both in English and in Spanish before several of his speeches.

Kennedy had another reason for going to Texas. He hoped to end the public squabbles between two Texas Democrats, Senator Ralph Yarborough, a liberal, and Governor John Connally, a conservative and a close friend of Vice President Lyndon Johnson, whom Yarborough also disliked. Such fighting was damaging to the Democratic party, and Kennedy wanted it stopped. He hoped his trip would force all three men to reconcile and unite behind his reelection efforts.

This goal was hard to achieve. When Kennedy arrived in San Antonio to begin his Texas tour, Yarborough refused to sit in Johnson's car during the presidential motorcade through the city. He refused again in Houston, their second stop. By the time the group reached Fort Worth, the president was angry with Yarborough. He demanded that the senator ride with Johnson on the way to the Hotel Texas, where they were to spend the night.

The next morning, November 22, 1963, Kennedy told his assistants to make sure Yarborough was in Johnson's car both on the way to the airport and in the motorcade through Dallas, where they were going next. "He'll ride with Johnson today or he'll walk," Kennedy said.[26] Then he went to make speeches before a large crowd gathered in the Hotel Texas parking lot and at a breakfast in the hotel dining room.

Meanwhile, the president's staff was trying to decide whether to leave the top off of the limousine he would be using that day in Dallas. Kennedy's car would be a specially equipped seven-passenger 1961 Lincoln Continental, with a fabric roof that could be left up or put down. It also had a top made of plastic, called the bubbletop, that could be bolted on instead of the fabric one. While the bubbletop was not bulletproof, it was a form of protection, because any bullet that managed to pierce the plastic would be turned on a different path within the car.

The president had never liked the bubbletop, which made it more difficult for people to see him and his wife as they drove by. However, he was willing to use it when the weather was poor. Someone called ahead to Dallas and found out that it was raining there, but only lightly, and the prediction was that the skies would clear. Those in charge of the car decided to leave the bubbletop off.

By this time the president and his wife were ready to leave the Hotel Texas and go to Fort Worth's Carswell Air Force Base, where they boarded *Air Force One* along with Governor Connally and his wife and Senator Yarborough. Vice President Johnson and his wife were on *Air Force Two*, which taxied down the runway first. Both planes were airborne a little after 11:20 A.M., on their way to Love Field in Dallas.

The city was only 33 miles (53 kilometers) away from Fort Worth, but it was very different in temperament. Dallas was a place controlled by ultraconservatives who did not believe in what Kennedy stood for, and it was often called the capital of the far right. The president warned his wife that their visit there could become violent. But he also told her, "If some-one wanted to shoot me from a window with a rifle, nobody can stop it. So why worry about it?"[27] He didn't want to let anything keep him from his speaking engagement in Dallas.

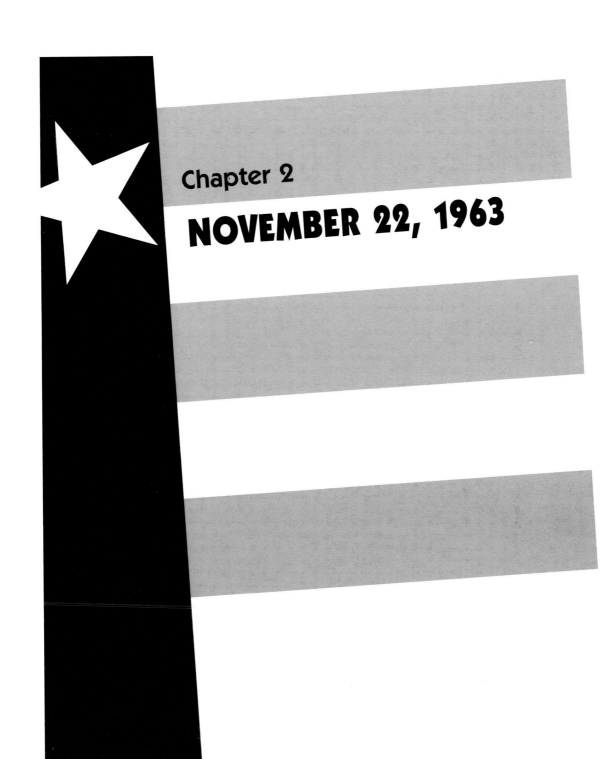

Chapter 2

NOVEMBER 22, 1963

On the morning of November 22, 1963, the *Dallas Morning News* contained several negative articles about Kennedy and the troubles between Yarborough and Johnson. It also held a full-page advertisement headed WELCOME MR. KENNEDY TO DALLAS that severely criticized the president.

"Because of your policy, thousands of Cubans have been imprisoned, are starving and being persecuted," the ad said. It went on to attack Kennedy on 11 other points, including his proposals for aid to various Communist countries, and accused Attorney General Robert Kennedy of being "soft on Communists, fellow-travelers, and ultra-leftists in America."[1] The ad was signed by "The American Fact-Finding Committee, Bernard Weissman, Chairman," but it was actually written by three members of the local John Birch Society, a right-wing organization, and paid for by wealthy Dallas businessmen.

In addition to the ad in the *Morning News*, for several days before Kennedy's visit someone had been circulating copies of an unsigned handbill accusing him of crimes against the United States government. This handbill included two photographs of the president, one front view and one side view, with the words WANTED FOR TREASON at the top. It then listed seven "treasonous activities" of the president, saying, among other things, that he had betrayed Cuba and supported communism.[2]

The handbill wasn't the only sign of trouble in Dallas. Just four days before Kennedy's election in 1960, an angry mob confronted Lyndon Johnson and his wife outside a local hotel. The protesters waved signs accusing Johnson of being a traitor to Texas and its conservative beliefs and spit on the pair as they tried to cross the street.

Later, there was even more violence. On October 24, 1963, only a month before Kennedy was scheduled to go to Texas, hecklers shouted at Adlai Stevenson, the U.S. ambassador to the United Nations, during his speech at a Dallas auditorium. Protesters then began walking up and down the aisles carrying upside-down U.S. flags. As the ambassador left the stage, a woman hit him with a sign, and later other protesters rocked his car to try to keep him from driving away. The event made the national news, and people began to talk about the climate of hatred in Dallas.

Agents of the Secret Service, a federal department charged with the duty of protecting the president, were particularly concerned about what had happened to Ambassador Stevenson. Prior to Kennedy's trip they obtained photographs of the protesters so they could make sure none of them was allowed into the Dallas Trade Mart, where the president would be making a luncheon speech; and on the morning of November 22, more than 200 Dallas police officers were assigned to guard the entrances and exits of the Trade Mart and check for signs of trouble.

Police also were stationed all along the streets that would take the president from Love Field through downtown Dallas to the Trade Mart. Because the local newspapers had published several versions of the route, a huge number of people turned out to watch the motorcade, and there was a great deal of noise and confusion. Foot patrolmen walked among the spectators, and motorcycle police tried to make sure the streets stayed clear. Other officers made sure no one stood on any overpasses.

At Love Field another large crowd had gathered to watch the president's plane land. They cheered when he finally stepped from *Air Force One* at a little after 11:40 A.M. *Air Force Two* had landed just moments before, so Vice President Johnson and his wife stood beside local officials waiting to greet the president. The Kennedys and the Connallys walked over to shake their hands, and someone handed Mrs. Connally a bouquet of yellow roses.

The sun was coming out from behind the clouds, and the day was so beautiful that no one regretted having left the bubbletop off the presidential limousine. The car sat nearby, ready for the president, but Kennedy and his wife instead went over to where the crowd stood cheering him from behind a chain link fence. They reached out to shake any hands that poked through, and Johnson and his wife soon were doing the same. For almost ten minutes the four of them greeted the people.

Governor Connally watched the crowd's excitement, listened to their cheers, and decided that Kennedy was popular in his state after all. Not wanting to seem against the president, he suddenly offered to let Senator Yarborough sit at the head table with him during the Trade Mart luncheon. Someone told this to President Kennedy, who said, "Terrific. That makes the whole trip worthwhile."[3]

Finally it was time to begin the motorcade, which would be led by four motorcycle policemen and a pilot car holding members of the Dallas police force. After them came four more motorcycle policemen whose job it was to keep people out of the way. The next car in the lineup was the lead car. It held the Dallas chief of police, the county sheriff, and a Secret Service agent, all of whom were to scan the crowds and buildings along the route for signs of trouble and take command if anything went wrong.

The president's convertible followed the lead car. Kennedy sat in the back seat next to Jackie, and Governor Connally and his wife were on jump seats ahead of them. The driver and front-seat passenger were both Secret Service agents. Normally the president's car would have had two additional agents running beside it, hopping onto the rear bumper and holding on to special handles when the car picked up speed, but Kennedy didn't like the way this looked so he ordered against it.

After the president's car came four more motorcycle policemen and a follow-up car holding eight Secret Service agents. Four of them rode on running boards, ready to jump off and protect the president's car whenever it stopped or slowed down to a crawl. Next in line was the vice pres-

The Kennedys are mobbed by well-wishers after landing at Love Field.

ident's four-door convertible. Johnson sat in the right rear seat, with his wife, Lady Bird, in the middle and Senator Yarborough on the left. The driver of the car was a Texas state highway patrolman, and a Secret Service agent sat beside him. Additional Secret Service agents rode in the vice president's follow-up car.

The rest of the 24-vehicle motorcade included still more Secret Service agents and members of the Dallas Police Department, the mayor of Dallas, Texas congressmen, and other important people. In addition, there were buses for members of the press and of the White House staff. Most of the vehicles were equipped with radios so that occupants could talk to one another over a special frequency that also connected them to Love Field and the Trade Mart.

As the drive got under way, the crowds along the route began cheer-

Moments before being shot, JFK smiles at the crowd. Governor and Mrs. Connally are in the front seat.

ing and waving, and everyone in the motorcade was astonished by how many people had shown up. "It was not at all as we envisioned," said one of Johnson's staff members later. "Just thousands of people. They outdid San Antonio and outdid Houston and outdid Fort Worth."[4] About 200,000 people watched the president pass. According to Governor Connally, "There was one little girl . . . who was carrying a sign saying, 'Mr. President, will you please stop and shake hands with me?' . . . He just told the driver to stop . . . and, of course, he was immediately mobbed by a bunch of youngsters."[5] Secret Service agents jumped off the running boards of the follow-up car and tried to hold back the crowd until the motorcade resumed. A little farther along the route, Kennedy saw a nun standing on a corner with some small children. Once more he stopped his car and shook hands.

Soon the motorcade began to run late because of these unplanned stops. The president's speech at the Trade Mart was set for 12:30 P.M., but at that time his car was still five minutes away, turning down Elm Street at a speed of about 11 miles (18 kilometers) per hour. On the left was a grassy area known as Dealey Plaza, and on the right stood a seven-story brick building called the Texas School Book Depository, where employees were hanging out of the windows to see the cars pass by. Next to the Depository was a little hill, or knoll, with some trees and a wooden picket fence. People stood on the knoll and all around Dealey Plaza, waving to President Kennedy and taking his picture.

Governor Connally's wife turned to Kennedy and said, "You sure can't say Dallas doesn't love you, Mr. President."[6] Suddenly there were several loud pops that sounded like someone setting off firecrackers. The presi-

John F. Kennedy Library

Onlookers dive for cover as the shots ring out on the grassy knoll next to the Texas School Book Depository.

In the first car, Jackie Kennedy tries to help her husband as Governor Connally (in profile at left) slumps forward after being shot.

dent clutched at his throat and slumped over. "We're hit!" shouted a Secret Service agent. Then Governor Connally felt a bullet pierce his back. "They're trying to kill us all!" he screamed.[7]

Secret Service Agent Clint Hill jumped off the running board of the follow-up car and ran toward the president's limousine. Before he could reach it, another bullet slammed into Kennedy's head. A terrified Jackie scrambled out of the car and onto its trunk. Agent Hill jumped on and shoved her back into her seat.

"Get down! Get down!" In the vice president's car, Agent Rufus Young-blood shouted at Johnson, then leaped over the front seat to push him to the floor. He shielded the vice president with his own body as the car sped from Dealey Plaza. "I heard over the radio system, 'Let's get out of here!'" Mrs. Johnson recalled. "The car accelerated terrifically fast—faster and faster."[8]

Kennedy's driver pushed his speed to almost 80 miles (128 kilometers) an hour and headed for Parkland Hospital, only four miles away. Within minutes the president's limousine had screeched to a stop in front of the emergency entrance, followed by the car carrying the Johnsons and Sena-tor Yarborough.

"The minute the car stopped, the Secret Service rushed at Johnson and formed a cordon around him," said Yarborough. "I heard one of them say 'Mr. President' to Johnson and I knew then Kennedy was dead. . . . I got up and walked up to the Kennedy car, and Mrs. Kennedy was sitting there with President Kennedy's head in her lap. I didn't say anything. There was too much agony. And I heard her say twice: 'They murdered my husband; they murdered my husband.'"[9]

At this point, however, no one else could believe that the president might not recover. Nurses and orderlies put him and Governor Connally on ambulance carts and rushed them inside to special trauma rooms, where doctors struggled to keep them alive. Meanwhile, Secret Service agents took Johnson to a small room in the hospital, drew the shades, and stood guard over him in the darkness.

Word of what had happened to the president began to spread. A reporter who had been in the motorcade, Merriman Smith of United Press International (UPI), used his car's radiophone to call his office with the news, and UPI sent his brief statement around the world: "Three shots were fired at President Kennedy's motorcade today in downtown Dal-las."[10] No one yet realized the extent of his injuries.

The crowd waiting to hear Kennedy's speech at the Trade Mart still did not know why he was late. People from the rear of the motorcade whose cars were without radios reached the luncheon confused as to why the president and vice president had sped off. As everyone waited and worried, rumors began to spread. Finally someone announced that the president was at Parkland Hospital, near death. "I was very, very upset, as were most of the others," said a Dallas attorney who attended the luncheon. "People were crying there and saying to other people they thought it was an assassination, a planned assassination by the so-called rightists, so-called Republicans. And they were saying that's gone too far."[11]

But government officials feared the attack on the president might be part of a plot by a foreign country to destroy the United States, and they wondered whether anyone else had been targeted. The secretary of state, the treasury secretary, and the secretary of commerce, along with several other important people, were on their way to Tokyo, Japan, for a trade conference. Concerned for their safety, the White House sent them a Teletype: "KENNEDY WOUNDED PERHAPS FATALLY BY ASSASSINS BULLET."[12] Their plane turned around immediately.

Back at Parkland Hospital doctors were operating on Governor Connally. He had bullet wounds in his back, chest, right wrist, and left thigh; his lung had collapsed and he had some fractured bones. Mrs. Connally sat with a hospital chaplain, praying her husband would recover. Finally the surgeons came out and told her that although Governor Connally's wounds were serious, eventually he would be all right.

The news for Mrs. Kennedy was not good. The president's head injury was massive and included severe brain damage. There was also a bullet hole in his throat. Had doctors ever turned Kennedy over, they would have seen still another wound in his upper back. They were certain there was no way for him to survive. "As soon as we knew we had nothing medical to do, we all backed off from the man with a reverence that one has for one's president," said one surgeon who was in the trauma room. "And we did not continue to be doctors from that point on. We became citizens again, and there were probably more tears shed in [the trauma] room than in the surrounding hundred miles."[13]

In the Catholic faith, when someone is about to die, a priest performs a ceremony called the last rites to forgive that person's soul for its sins. Doctors agreed not to pronounce Kennedy dead until his wife had found a priest, and the Reverend Oscar Huber came to give the last rites. "During this most trying ordeal, the perfect composure maintained by Mrs. Kennedy was beyond comprehension," said Huber. "I will never forget the blank stare in her eyes and the signs of agony on her face."[14] Mrs. Kennedy then gave her husband a last kiss and slipped her wedding ring from her finger onto his. Only a half hour after he had been smiling and waving in front of the Texas School Book Depository, President John Fitzgerald Kennedy was officially pronounced dead.

Secret Service agents went to notify Johnson of Kennedy's death. They also urged him to leave Dallas. He was now the de facto president, meaning that as soon as he was sworn in, he would have full executive powers, and they wanted him out of the city before news of President Kennedy's death was announced to the public. Johnson and his wife agreed to go, on the condition that Mrs. Kennedy accompany them. "I'm not leaving without Jack," she said.[15] Mr. and Mrs. Johnson went on ahead to Love Field to wait for her while Kennedy's aides tried to locate a casket.

On board *Air Force One*, Johnson called the White House to get advice about his swearing-in ceremony. The attorney general, President Kennedy's brother Robert, told him to find a judge in Dallas who could administer the oath of office immediately. Johnson then phoned the office of U.S. District Judge Sarah T. Hughes. When he was told she was out, Johnson said, "I want Sarah Hughes to meet me at the airport. President Kennedy is dead, and I want her to swear me in. I don't care what you have to do—find her."[16] He hung up the phone and sat down to wait. Someone turned on the television, where a reporter was just announcing the president's death.

Kennedy's aides were still at Parkland Hospital, arguing with a local medical examiner. "There has been a homicide here," the man said. "You won't be able to remove the body. We will take it down to the mortuary for an autopsy."[17] The aides demanded to be allowed out of the building with the casket, and the medical examiner began shouting at them. "We can't release it!" he yelled. "A violent death requires a postmortem!"[18] Finally the medical examiner called in policemen and a judge to enforce his demand.

Secret Service agents began to surround the casket. "These people say you can't go," one of the policemen told them, referring to the judge and the medical examiner.[19] The agents pushed the casket past him. They carted it out the door as the judge phoned the district attorney, who said he did not object to the removal of the body.

The agents loaded the president's body into a hearse for the trip to Love Field. Mrs. Kennedy climbed in beside it, her dress and gloves caked with her husband's blood. Earlier, an aide had tried to get her to clean herself up. "It's his blood," she said. "I do not want to remove this. I want them to see what they've done to him."[20]

Agents ran to the front of the car and jumped in. They rushed Kennedy's body to *Air Force One* and put it onto the plane as quickly as possible, certain that Dallas officials would change their minds about the autopsy. Then they asked Johnson for permission to take off immediately. The vice president refused. He insisted they wait for Judge Hughes and the swearing-in ceremony.

Finally, just before 2:30, Judge Hughes arrived. The president's staff invited select members of the press onto the plane to witness the oath of office alongside Mrs. Johnson, Mrs. Kennedy, and some of the people who had served President Kennedy during his three years in office. When Hughes began the ceremony, "her voice cracked, and her hands were shaking," said one witness. "She was obviously rather in a state of…near hysteria."[21] A photographer snapped pictures as Lyndon Baines Johnson became the 36th president of the United States. The mood was somber and there were few congratulations. Once Judge Hughes had left the plane, the new president gave his first command: "Let's get airborne."[22]

Public officials in Washington, D.C., began heading to Andrews Air Force Base, where the plane would land. World leaders phoned the White House and *Air Force One* to express their condolences, and President John-

John F. Kennedy Library

Lyndon Johnson takes the oath of office from Judge Sarah T. Hughes on board Air Force One.

son returned some of these calls while in the air. He also contacted President Kennedy's mother to tell her of his deep sorrow over her son's death. "We're grieving with you," he said.[23]

Nearby, Mrs. Kennedy was sitting quietly, alone, still in her blood-stained clothes. After a while the president's personal physician approached her to discuss her husband's autopsy. "The doctors must remove the bullet," he said. "The authorities must know the type. It becomes evidence."[24] Mrs. Kennedy was opposed to the idea of an autopsy, but at last she agreed to the procedure, which would be performed at Bethesda Naval Hospital.

Finally the plane landed. The sun had just set, and Washington was in darkness. On the runway, in the glare of artificial lighting, an honor guard stood at attention and dignitaries waited in silence. The nation watched via television as the casket was lowered from *Air Force One*. Robert Kennedy was there to help Mrs. Kennedy, who followed her husband's body into the ambulance that would carry it to Bethesda. President Johnson emerged from the plane and stepped up to the microphones. "This is a sad time for all people," he said. "We have suffered a loss that cannot be weighed. For me it is a deep personal tragedy." He went on to add, "I will do my best. That is all I can do."[25]

The entire nation was in mourning. "I wept openly for the first time in ten years, for the first time since my own father died," said Georgia farmer Jimmy (James Earl) Carter, who later became president of the United States himself.[26] One newsman later recalled, "I remember standing in the editor's office . . . when the announcer gave the definite news that the president indeed was dead. I heard a gasp and a male reporter was sobbing. I had never seen that before."[27]

America's grief soon spread across the world. In London the bell at Westminster Abbey tolled in memory of President Kennedy. In Vienna the opera was canceled; in Paris the shops were closed. In Copenhagen thousands laid flowers in front of the American Embassy, and in West Berlin students marched through the night carrying lighted torches. Even Cuban premier Fidel Castro, when he heard the news, seemed upset. "This is bad news," he said over and over. Then he added, "Everything is changed.... I'll tell you one thing: at least Kennedy was an enemy to whom we had become accustomed."[28]

Meanwhile, Dallas police were busy trying to figure out exactly what had happened and why. They had already captured the man they believed was the assassin, and they felt they were well on their way to solving the crime. "I can tell you that this case is cinched—that this man killed the president. There's no question in my mind about it," said the Dallas police captain in charge of the investigation.[29] He did not know that the mystery of who killed President Kennedy was just beginning.

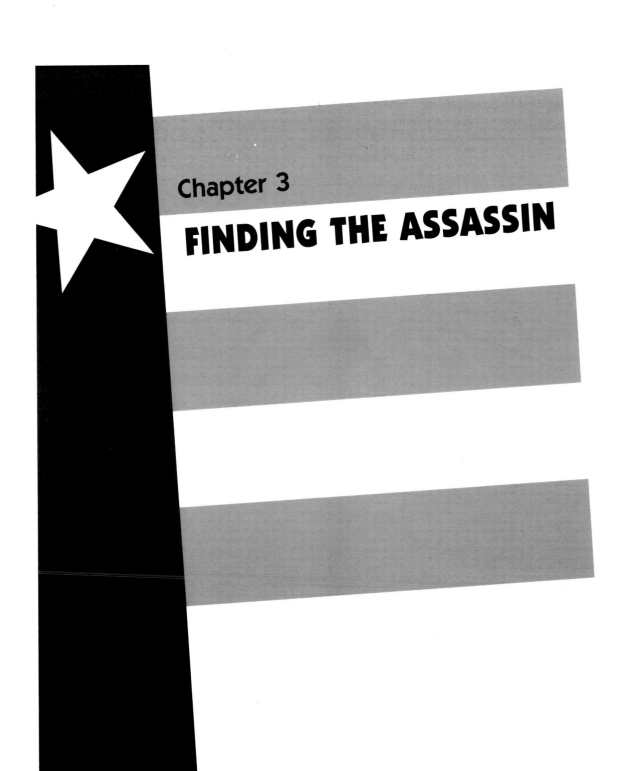

Chapter 3

FINDING THE ASSASSIN

At the moment of the assassination, people in Dealey Plaza had started screaming and running or dropping to the ground in fear of being shot themselves. But once the motorcade had sped away, everyone began to look around to see who had done the shooting. Witnesses and policemen ran up the nearby grassy knoll and behind the wooden picket fence. Other officers headed to an underpass to search for suspects. Then 15-year-old Amos Euins told police he had seen a man with a rifle in a window of the School Book Depository.[1] Another witness, Howard Brennan, described the man as being white, slender, and in his early 30s.[2]

Marrion Baker, a motorcycle policeman from the end of the motorcade, was already at the Depository. Certain the gunfire had come from there, he had jumped off his motorcycle and run inside only seconds after the president was shot. Then he and the building manager, Roy Truly, ran up the stairs. On the second floor Officer Baker saw a man entering a lunchroom door and confronted him. It was less than two minutes after the shooting.

Baker immediately noticed that the man was not out of breath and had no weapon. "Do you know this man?" the officer asked Truly. "Yes, he works for me," Truly answered. Officer Baker nodded and ran from the lunchroom with Truly following behind. On the fifth floor the two men took the elevator to the seventh floor and then the roof.[3]

Once Baker and Truly had gone, the man they had seen, 24-year-old Lee Harvey Oswald, left the lunchroom and walked through an office on his way to the front stairway. A woman who watched him pass told him the president had been shot. He mumbled something and kept going.[4] Forty-three minutes later he would be seen entering his rooming house, only to leave again almost immediately.[5]

Right after Oswald left the Depository, two officers were stationed in front of the building with instructions to keep people from going in or coming out. Other officers were supposed to watch the rear door, but a member of the Secret Service who arrived at the Depository 25 minutes after the assassination found it unguarded.[6] Inside he found investigators conducting a careful search, looking behind stacked book boxes and anywhere else an assassin might hide. Baker and Truly had finished checking the roof and were back on the ground floor, where police were gathering together all employees for questioning. Truly noticed that Oswald was missing from this group, and he reported this to Police Captain Will Fritz.[7]

An officer searching the sixth floor found an odd arrangement of boxes in the southeast corner. They were stacked higher than normal, and when he squeezed behind them he found a window with a perfect view of the street below. Beneath that window someone had placed a shorter stack of boxes on which a gun barrel could have rested. A nearby box could have been used as a seat. The officer saw three empty rifle shells on the floor and thought he had discovered the spot from which the assassin had fired.

An investigator from the Dallas Crime Laboratory collected the shells, dusted for fingerprints, and took photographs. Other detectives discovered a homemade bag whose brown wrapping paper and tape were the same as the kind used by Depository employees. At first, detectives couldn't figure out what this bag might have been used for, but when they found a rifle amid a stack of cartons, they thought they knew. Disassembled, the gun would have fit perfectly into the cone-shaped bag.

Outside the Depository building, police were also working to find the

Investigators peer out the window from which the shots were fired that killed JFK.

assassin. They questioned some vagrants and workers at a nearby railroad yard and interviewed witnesses in Dealey Plaza. Soon they were broadcasting a description of the gunman to all patrol cars in the area.

Driving through a residential neighborhood in the Oak Cliff section of town, Officer John Tippit noticed someone who fit that description. When he stopped his patrol car and got out, the man fired at him four times with a revolver. As Tippit lay dying on the ground, the killer ejected the bullet shells from his gun, tossed them into some bushes, reloaded, and jogged off down the street as one of the witnesses to the killing used the radio in the patrol car to call for help.[8]

Police broadcast a description of this gunman, and an officer immediately radioed in that he had seen a man fitting that description run into the nearby public library. Officers raced to surround the building. When they got there, they learned that it was only a library employee hurrying inside to tell his co-workers about the president's death.[9]

Several blocks away the manager of an Oak Cliff shoe shop, Johnny Brewer, was listening to a radio news broadcast about a police officer who had been shot in the area. Just then he noticed a man hurrying past his store window. As a police car drove by, the man stopped and turned to hide his face. Brewer decided that this was suspicious, and he went outside to see where the man was going. When the stranger went up the street and into the Texas Theater without stopping to buy a ticket, Brewer alerted the cashier, who became excited and called the police. "We have your man," she told them. "Every time the sirens go by he ducks."[10]

Police surrounded the theater within minutes. Inside, Brewer told them about the stranger and pointed him out, and they began ordering people to stand one by one to be searched. Officer Nick McDonald started to check the man Brewer had indicated. According to McDonald, "As soon as I got to him—I was just inches from him—I said, 'Get on your feet.' He stood up, and he said, 'Well, it's all over now.' He was bringing his hands up at this point. . . . Suddenly [he] made a fist . . . hit me between the eyes . . . and in the same motion drew a pistol from his waist."[11] The officer hit back and grabbed the gun. Three other officers rushed forward, and after a struggle they handcuffed the suspect, dragged him from the theater, and put him in a patrol car. "I don't know why you're doing this to me," the man said. "The only thing I have done is carry a pistol in a movie." "You've done a lot more," one of the officers answered. "You've killed a policeman."[12]

At police headquarters Detective Gus Rose was assigned to interview the man, who wouldn't even tell him his name. Detective Rose looked through the man's wallet. In it were several papers with the name Lee Oswald on them, including a U.S. Marine Corps certificate of service and a Department of Defense identification card. There also were two cards with the name Alek Hidell on them—a Selective Service System card with a photograph of Oswald on it and another certificate of service from the marines. Rose asked the man whether he was Oswald or Hidell. He answered, "You're the detective. You figure it out."[13]

Captain Fritz walked in and told Rose he wanted him to find an employee who was missing from the School Book Depository, someone named Lee Harvey Oswald. A stunned Rose said the man was already there. Captain Fritz had Oswald brought into his office and began to question him. No record of the conversation was made.

Word of Oswald's capture spread through police headquarters. James Bookhout, an agent from the Federal Bureau of Investigation (FBI), learned of the capture and notified the Dallas FBI office. There FBI Agent James Hosty immediately recognized Oswald's name. He told his boss he knew a great deal about this man, and his boss sent him to help Captain Fritz with Oswald's questioning.

Agent Hosty had been assigned by the FBI to keep a record of Oswald's activities but claimed he had never actually met Oswald. He had personally questioned Oswald's wife, Marina, who lived apart from her husband in Irving, a Dallas suburb. Marina spoke very little English, and her friend Ruth Paine acted as her translator. During Hosty's conversations with her, Marina supposedly made it clear that she wanted the U.S. government to leave her husband alone.[14] The Russian-born Marina was afraid she might be forced to leave the country because of Oswald's involvement in the Fair Play for Cuba Committee, a group that supported Castro and his Communist regime.

Oswald had been interested in both communism and Marxism all his life. As a boy, he frequently argued politics and had trouble getting along with others. He also kept skipping school. At age 17 he joined the Marine Corps, where he talked back to superiors and was reprimanded often. He was court-martialed once for insulting an officer and another time for possessing an unregistered .22-caliber pistol; his punishment was confinement and hard labor.

Finally Oswald asked to be removed from active duty, claiming that his widowed mother had been injured at work and needed his help. The marines approved his discharge and sent him home to Fort Worth, but only three days later he traveled to New Orleans and booked passage on a ship headed for Europe. From there he went to the Soviet Union. He had learned to speak Russian while in the marines, and he felt that the Soviet government would easily accept him. He wanted to defect.

To Oswald's dismay, Soviet officials told him he would have to return to the United States. Eventually they changed their minds, but they still did not grant him Soviet citizenship. They sent Oswald to live in Minsk and gave him a job as a metalworker in a radio and television factory.

At the factory he found it no easier to follow orders, and he began to dis-

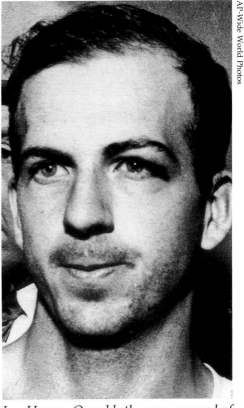

AP-Wide World Photos

Lee Harvey Oswald, the man accused of assassinating President John F. Kennedy

like the Russian way of life. He felt it unfair that Communist party members were treated better than everybody else. He complained about the many political meetings he was made to attend. In his diary he wrote about missing nightclubs, bowling alleys, and other places where people could have fun. He hated the lack of freedom in his new country. "I have had enough," he wrote.[15] A short time later he met and married Marina Prusakova, the niece of a prominent Communist official, and began making arrangements with the U.S. Embassy in Moscow for the two of them to move to the United States. He borrowed money from the U.S. government to pay for his return.[16]

Oswald arrived back in Texas in July 1962. He got a job in Fort Worth as a metalworker, but in October he quit and went to Dallas to work for a photography firm. Unable to get along with co-workers, he was fired the following April. He then moved to New Orleans to work as a greaser and oiler of coffee processing machines. Again he was fired. By this time he had become involved with the Fair Play for Cuba Committee. He was seen handing out pro-Castro leaflets, and some said that in September he tried to enter Cuba from Mexico but was denied a visa. He ended up in Dallas, where he tried, unsuccessfully, to find work at another photographic firm and finally got a job at the Texas School Book Depository.

Now Oswald sat in a third-floor office at police headquarters being questioned by Captain Fritz, FBI agents Bookhout and Hosty, and several other local and federal officials. Out in the corridor more than 100 newsmen were crowded together amid two large television cameras and countless lights, cables, and microphones. Every time someone involved in the investigation walked by, reporters began shouting questions. It was difficult to get past them without being jostled or grabbed at. No one could control them, and their numbers kept growing.

Officers were supposed to check the credentials of everyone in the corridor, but according to the assistant chief of police, "anybody could come up with a plausible reason for going to one of the third floor bureaus and was able to get in."[17] The situation was becoming dangerous for the prisoner, but police did not tighten security and took no special measures to safeguard Oswald's life. In their minds he had killed the president of the United States, as well as a fellow officer, and they were completely focused on proving him guilty.

Chapter 4

QUESTIONS UNANSWERED

Police interviewed Oswald off and on between the afternoon of November 22 and the morning of November 24. Sometimes they allowed him to rest for a while in his cell on the fifth floor, and other times they took him down to the basement, where various witnesses were waiting to pick him out of a lineup. Each time he went to the jail elevator, Oswald had to pass the jostling, shouting reporters and photographers.

In Captain Fritz's office Oswald was asked about his activities at the School Book Depository and his whereabouts between the time of the assassination and his capture at the Texas Theater. He answered some of the questions but not others.

Oswald did discuss his job at the Depository, telling investigators that he was usually on the second floor but that his work took him to all floors. He said that when the president was shot, he was on the first floor having his lunch. After that he went up to buy a soda at the second-floor lunchroom, where he saw Roy Truly, the building manager, and Officer Baker. Asked why he left the building, Oswald said it was because "there was so much excitement all around, I figured that there would be no more work."[1]

Oswald said he did not own a rifle but did go to his rooming house in Oak Cliff that day to get his revolver. "You know how boys do when they have a gun," he explained. "They just carry it."[2] He said that his wife and two little girls lived in the house of a friend, Mrs. Ruth Paine, and that he visited them every weekend, even though he did not own a car.[3]

Oswald admitted he was a member of the Fair Play for Cuba Committee but denied belonging to the Communist party.[4] "Why did you carry that pistol into the show?" Captain Fritz abruptly asked him. "I told you why," Oswald answered. "I don't want to talk about it anymore."[5]

Oswald requested an attorney. "You can have one anytime you want," Captain Fritz said. Oswald wanted John Abt, an attorney in New York, but he didn't have the money to call him. "Call him collect or you can have another lawyer if you want," Captain Fritz told him. Yet he did not allow Oswald to use a phone, and the questioning continued.[6]

Agent Hosty asked Oswald if he had ever been to the Soviet Union. Oswald answered calmly that he had. But when Hosty asked if he had taken a trip to Mexico, Oswald said he had not and became upset. "I know you! I know you!" he shouted at Hosty. Oswald told the other investigators that Hosty had gone to his home and threatened his wife, making her feel that she would be sent back to the Soviet Union if her husband did anything wrong.[7]

Oswald insisted that his only crime was carrying a gun into a theater and resisting arrest. He denied assassinating the president or killing Officer Tippit. But Dallas police felt the evidence was beginning to suggest otherwise. At their lineups an eyewitness to Tippit's murder identified Oswald. So did some of those who had seen a man with a rifle in the Depository window. However, none of them was absolutely certain it was Oswald—not even Howard Brennan, who had given a detailed description of the man to police.

"I told them I could not make a positive identification," Brennan later explained, but he said that he did this on purpose, because he was afraid. "I believed at that time, and I still believe it was a Communist activity, and I felt like there hadn't been more than one eyewitness, and if it got to be a known fact that I was an eyewitness, my family or I, either one, might not be safe."[8]

Fifteen-year-old Amos Euins also could not identify Oswald as the per-

Crowds outside the Dallas courthouse wait to catch a glimpse of Lee Harvey Oswald. In the background is the Texas School Book Depository, from where the shots were fired.

son he had seen shooting at the president. He said he wasn't even sure whether the gunman was white or black.[9]

Police also took statements from employees at the Depository. One man said Oswald had been on the sixth floor just 35 minutes before the assassination.[10] However, an employee who had finished eating his lunch there 25 minutes later said he hadn't seen Oswald.[11] Someone from the fifth floor said he had heard the bullet shells drop onto the floor above. Yet other workers inside the building said that as they ran downstairs after the shots were fired, no one else was in the stairwell and the elevator never moved.[12]

Other witnesses told about Oswald's activities after he left the Depository. Using their testimony, police decided that Oswald had walked seven blocks to a bus stop, taken a bus that went back past the Depository, left the bus, gotten into a cab, traveled to Oak Cliff, and been let out a short distance from his rooming house.[13] However, the bus driver would eventually say he was mistaken about his passenger being Oswald, and the descriptions other witnesses gave of Oswald's clothing didn't match.[14]

A woman who knew Oswald said she had seen him on the bus and he wore no jacket.[15] But the cabdriver who had taken Oswald to Oak Cliff said he had on a blue jacket exactly like the one police later found at the Depository building. Officials concluded that the cabdriver "was in error....Oswald could not possibly have been wearing the blue jacket during the [cab ride]."[16] Witnesses to Officer Tippit's murder said the gunman wore a light-colored jacket. One was found near the site of the murder and identified by Marina Oswald as belonging to her husband, but none of the witnesses could state with absolute certainty that it was the same jacket. To confuse matters even more, the housekeeper at Oswald's rooming house said he had left there in a dark jacket.[17]

Another piece of evidence in dispute was a brown paper sack that Oswald had carried with him to work that morning. According to a co-worker who had driven him to the Depository, "it was a package just roughly about two feet long" that Oswald had placed on the backseat of the car and said held curtain rods.[18] The man's sister had seen the bag, too. "[Oswald] was carrying a package in a sort of heavy brown bag, heavier than a grocery bag," she stated.[19] Oswald said that these people were "mistaken." He told police that the bag had been a lunch sack and that he had kept it on his lap during the drive.[20] Detectives decided it was the same bag they had found on the sixth floor, even though the witnesses insisted it was too short to hold the disassembled rifle.[21]

Inside the bag investigators discovered a single brown fiber and several light green ones, and on the outside a fingerprint and palm print that matched Oswald's. Oswald's palm prints were also on the boxes near the sixth-floor window and, according to one expert but not another, on the barrel of the rifle police said they had discovered at the Depository, an Italian Mannlicher-Carcano with a crooked sight.[22] Four experts later stated that this 6.5-millimeter rifle had fired the bullets that killed the president and wounded Governor Connally. Moreover, the gun bore a few cotton fibers similar to those in the shirt Oswald was wearing when arrested at the Texas Theater.[23]

Police traced the manufacturer of the Mannlicher-Carcano rifle and learned that the weapon had been shipped by a firearms company to a Chicago sporting goods store. The store then sold it by mail to someone named A. Hidell. The rifle was shipped to a Dallas post office box rented to Oswald. The handwriting on the order form matched Oswald's. Another mail-order form had been used to purchase Oswald's revolver, which had also been sent to A. J. Hidell at the same post office box.

"[Oswald] denied that the rifle was his," said Secret Service Agent Forrest Sorrels, who was present during some of Oswald's questioning. "He denied knowing or using the name of A. Hidell, or Alek Hidell....He still maintained an arrogant, defiant attitude....He gave me the impression of lying to Captain Fritz and deliberately doing so."[24]

Police searched the home where Marina was staying to gather more evidence against Oswald. Most important were two photographs of him holding a rifle that closely resembled the one from the Depository. In the garage there was a green-and-brown blanket in which Marina said her husband kept a gun. The fibers in this blanket were similar to those found in

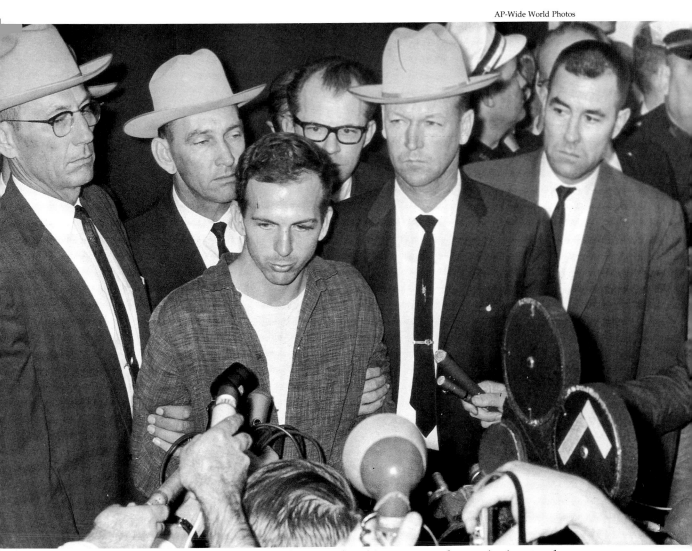

Lee Harvey Oswald is brought out after his arrest and questioning to show reporters that police had not harmed him.

the homemade paper bag. Marina said that Oswald had spent some time in the garage the night before the assassination, having come to visit her unexpectedly. The next morning he left behind his wedding ring and his wallet, which contained $170.[25]

By 7:00 P.M. on the night of November 22, investigators felt they had enough evidence to officially charge Oswald with the murder of Officer Tippit; four hours later they also indicted him for the assassination of President Kennedy. But in 1963 it was not a federal offense to kill the president of the United States, only to threaten him. "The most we could charge him with is assault on the president and the maximum penalty is five years," said one federal official.[26] The Dallas district attorney's office would have to handle the prosecution.

Police booked Oswald and finally allowed him to place a collect call to attorney John Abt. Abt's office refused to accept the charges.[27] Later, District Attorney Henry Wade tried to contact Abt himself. "[Abt] said he was not going to handle the case, was not interested in it," Wade explained. "I got the president of the Dallas Bar and the president of the Dallas Criminal Bar to go down and see [Oswald]. They reported [that Oswald] said he didn't want them."[28] Oswald was brought back to Captain Fritz for more questioning. Fritz showed him one of the photographs found at Mrs. Paine's house. According to Inspector Thomas Kelley, who was there at the time, Oswald "sneered at them, saying that they were false photographs."[29] He said that the face was his but the body was not and "got into a long argument with Captain Fritz about his knowledge of photography."[30] Kelley added that Oswald insisted "that at the proper time he would show the photographs were fakes."[31] Marina would eventually tell police that she

AP-Wide World Photos

Jack Ruby, the nightclub owner who shot and killed Lee Harvey Oswald

had shot these pictures in the backyard of an apartment house where she and Oswald once lived.[32]

While Oswald was being questioned, the crowd in the third-floor corridor grew larger and louder. One of the people there was Jack Ruby, a Dallas nightclub owner. Ruby had been seen at Parkland Hospital right after the wounded president was taken there, and some even claimed he was at Dealey Plaza just before the assassination.[33]

Ruby was also at a special press conference held in the basement of police headquarters the night Oswald was arrested. Police brought Oswald before reporters and photographers to prove he hadn't been beaten up or killed. Then they took him away again, and District Attorney Wade started answering questions. Asked whether Oswald was a Communist, Wade said that Oswald had been a member of the Free Cuba Movement. Jack Ruby corrected him from the crowd. "No," Ruby said. "It's the Fair Play for Cuba Committee." Afterward the district attorney asked Ruby what he was doing there. "I know all these fellows," Ruby answered.[34]

Ruby did indeed know many Dallas police officers personally. In the nightclubs he owned he often gave them free drinks, and at headquarters he sometimes stopped by with sandwiches or doughnuts. He had organized a benefit to help a policeman's widow pay for her dead husband's funeral, and he had attended services for others killed in the line of duty. Some said he did these things because he truly respected and admired the police, but others believed it was to get special treatment for his clubs. In any case, many Dallas police officers accepted Ruby's generosity and enjoyed his company.[35]

Ruby also associated with members of organized crime. He once worked for a Chicago union run by the mob, and for a while he sold tip sheets at racetracks in Los Angeles and San Francisco. One of his closest friends in Dallas had been convicted of trying to bribe the sheriff. Another friend, a professional gambler, paid for Ruby to visit Cuba in 1959, supposedly to check out a gambling house there. Ruby had taken additional trips to Mexico, Las Vegas, New Orleans, New York, and Chicago.[36]

Wherever he went, Ruby usually carried a gun under his suitcoat. He kept large amounts of cash in his pockets—sometimes as much as several thousand dollars—as well as in the trunk of his car and at his Oak Cliff apartment, only a mile from Oswald's rooming house. Frequently in trouble with the Internal Revenue Service (IRS) over unreported income and late tax payments, Ruby didn't use banks, because they might have turned his money over to the IRS.[37]

Ruby had been arrested several times. His crimes included carrying a concealed weapon and breaking the liquor laws. Despite this, at headquarters Dallas police allowed him to come and go as he pleased. They did nothing to stop him as he walked into the basement on the morning of November 24 to watch Oswald's transfer to the county jail.[38]

Only the night before, the local FBI office had received an anonymous threat that a group of 100 to 200 men were going to try to kill Oswald.[39] "I have always felt it was Ruby who made the call," Captain Fritz said years later. But according to Dallas Chief of Police Jesse Curry, "We really expected trouble, if we had trouble, from a group of people and not an individual."[40]

The phone threat made some officials wonder whether Oswald should be transferred in secret. "I suggested to the chief that we double-cross the media and take Oswald out on the first floor and put him in a car and take him down to the County Jail," said Detective James Leavelle. He told Chief Curry, "We can be down there before anybody knows we've even started with him."[41] The chief rejected this idea, saying, "I told the people that I would transfer him and let the television people film it.…I'm going to keep my word."[42] That night Chief Curry told reporters, "I believe if you are back here by ten o'clock [tomorrow morning] you will be back in time to observe anything you care to observe."[43]

Dallas police made arrangements to drive Oswald to the county jail in an armored truck. But on the morning of the transfer, Captain Fritz decided that Oswald should go in a car instead, and Chief Curry agreed with him.[44] Detectives and Secret Service agents suggested that they wait to move Oswald until a time when no reporters were around. "We cannot do that,"

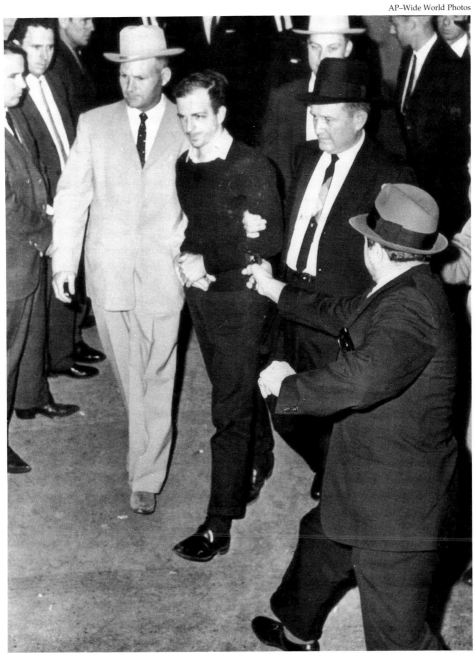

Jack Ruby steps forward to shoot Lee Harvey Oswald as police escort him from the jail to a waiting car.

Curry said. "We are obligated to the press."[45] He ordered the detectives to take Oswald out through the basement of the building, and he allowed reporters access to the area.[46]

"The only time I saw [Oswald] scared was when we went up to get him out of jail to transfer him…and I told him there had been threats on his life," said one detective.[47] From his cell Oswald was taken to Captain Fritz's office for one last questioning session. He still did not admit to having killed anybody, and he denied being a Communist. "I am a Marxist," he explained. He also said that he didn't think much of the Bible. "I have no faith," he stated.[48]

Oswald was supposed to be transferred at 10:00 A.M., but it was after 11:00 when Chief Curry came to Captain Fritz's office and said it was time to go. Oswald demanded a disguise, complaining that because of the press, everyone knew what clothes he was wearing. A detective gave him an old black sweater.[49]

Down in the basement more than 70 police officers and over 40 reporters were waiting for Oswald. Somehow Jack Ruby managed to join them. There was a great deal of confusion, and the cars were farther away than police had intended. Oswald would have to walk some distance before getting into a vehicle.

Detectives led Oswald out into the basement parking area and past the reporters as television cameras began broadcasting his appearance live across the nation. Suddenly Jack Ruby stepped from the crowd, pulled out a gun, and fired one shot directly into Oswald's abdomen. Oswald crumpled and fell to the ground.

Detectives rushed to arrest Ruby. Others carried Oswald back inside the jail offices and called for an ambulance. He was taken to Parkland Hospital, where at 1:07 P.M. he was pronounced dead. Only one hour earlier President Kennedy's coffin had begun its funeral procession from the White House to the Capitol building. The two men would be buried on the same day, but the world would not mourn Oswald's death as it did Kennedy's.

Chapter 5

A NATION GRIEVES

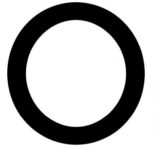n the morning of November 23, President Kennedy's body was taken from Bethesda Naval Hospital to the East Room of the White House. Jackie Kennedy had chosen this room for her husband's lying-in-state because President Abraham Lincoln's body had lain there after his assassination in 1865.

Jackie Kennedy had read everything she could about Lincoln's funeral, and she used it to help plan her husband's. She decorated the East Room just as it had been when Lincoln's body rested there, with black curtains hanging from the windows and a flag draped over the coffin. "All of that was done from pictures and drawings and renditions of Lincoln lying there," said State Department Chief of Protocol Angier Duke. "It was very impressive, very awesome, in a very majestic way."[1] She also wanted a black, riderless horse to be led behind the president's casket during his funeral procession, just as in Lincoln's procession.[2]

She chose her husband's gravesite because of its relationship to the Lincoln Memorial. "[The Kennedy family] picked a site that was in line with the center of the Lincoln Memorial and the center of the Lincoln Bridge and the Lee Custis Mansion that sits on the hill above the grave," said one army engineer. "It had to be on the center line of those three things. We took a surveying instrument and lined it up."[3] The president would be

Surrounded by mourners, Kennedy's coffin lies in state in the Capitol Rotunda as Jackie and Caroline kneel to pay their respects.

buried in Arlington National Cemetery in northern Virginia, a place he had visited only a few weeks earlier. At that time he had said, "This is the most perfect view of Washington. I could stay here forever."[4]

Four men, one from each branch of military service, stood silent guard over his body as it lay in the East Room. Two hours before dawn on November 23, a brief service was held there for the White House staff, and later in the morning, a priest said a Catholic mass in the East Room before

Jackie, Caroline, and John, Jr. leave the Capitol with members of the Kennedy family after the memorial service for JFK.

Kennedy family members and close friends.[5]

All across the country people were holding their own memorials for the president. At Parkland Hospital Governor Connally's family and friends attended a small service. Elsewhere in Dallas, churches were filled with mourners, and flowers covered the grassy knoll at Dealey Plaza. "On Saturday the whole city was in shock," said one pastor. "Everyone was walking around numb. You'd drive down the street and see people walking, with their eyes to the ground."[6]

The next morning Jackie and Robert Kennedy went to the East Room to take one last look at the president's body. Inside his coffin they placed three letters, one from Jackie, one from Caroline, and one from John-John, even though his letter contained only scribblings. Jackie also put in two of her husband's favorite possessions, a pair of gold cuff links and a scrimshaw with the presidential seal on it. Robert added his own PT-109 tiepin, which he had gotten during his brother's presidential campaign, and an engraved silver rosary.[7] Finally the coffin was closed.

The casket was then carried outside, taken down the steps of the White House, and placed carefully on a two-wheeled cart called a caisson, which was pulled by a team of pure white horses. Accompanying the caisson was a special honor guard, a national color detail, a police marching unit, and a detail of navy enlisted men. Even with all these people, there was no sound except the beat of muffled drums.

Also in the procession was a man leading an all-black horse. The animal, whose name was Black Jack, pranced along nervously without a rider. On his back was a saddle with a riding boot turned backward in each stirrup, symbolizing a leader gone forever.

Thousands of people stood quietly along the streets of Washington to watch the slow procession pass by. Those who couldn't be there in person saw it on television. They followed the caisson's progress to the Capitol building, where a 21-gun salute was fired in the president's honor. Then a group of honorary pallbearers carried the casket up the steps of the Capitol Rotunda. When they reached the top, the Navy Band played "Hail to the Chief." After that the casket was carried inside, where countless government officials and other important people had already gathered to pay their last respects to President Kennedy.

Senate Majority Leader Mike Mansfield began the brief memorial service. "There was a man marked with the scars of his love of country," he said, "a body active with the surge of a life far, far from spent and, in a moment, it was no more."[8] Chief Justice Earl Warren and House Speaker John McCormack also spoke about President Kennedy and what he had given his country. Then Jackie and Caroline Kennedy knelt and kissed the flag draped over the coffin. "It was a very emotional moment for all of us," said an observer.[9]

Once the Kennedy family and other dignitaries had left, an honor guard was placed around the coffin and the Rotunda was opened to the public. All afternoon and evening thousands of people came to pay their respects to the president. The line stretched on and on, and many waited hours to get in. Although officials had planned to end the viewing at 8:00 P.M., they decided not to turn anyone away. The mourners continued coming to Capitol Hill throughout the night.

Meanwhile, world leaders were arriving in Washington, D.C., for another ceremony the following day, when the casket would be carried to St. Matthew's Cathedral for services and then on to Arlington National Cemetery. The White House staff was kept busy all night meeting people at the airport and arranging for their stay in the city. Other officials were at the cemetery, making sure everything was ready there. Jackie Kennedy had requested that an eternal flame, similar to one she had seen in France, be constructed for her husband's grave, and workers had to struggle to finish it on time.

At 9:45 A.M. on Monday, November 25, the final funeral procession began. The president's casket was carried down the Rotunda steps and placed back on the caisson. Once more the team of white horses pulled it through the streets of Washington, and again the riderless horse, Black Jack, was led behind the casket. "[The horse's] occasional random movements seemed to express the futility of it all," said one witness.[10] After

John F. Kennedy Library

Kennedy's coffin is carried through the streets of Washington followed by a riderless black horse.

Black Jack came world leaders, government officials, and Kennedy family members, all walking on foot to the beat of muffled drums. Televisions across the world, even in the Soviet Union, broadcast this procession into homes and churches, where many people had gathered to watch the services together.

Once the caisson had passed the White House and reached St. Matthew's Cathedral, the coffin was carried inside for a huge funeral service. The Mass was said in Latin, but at the end Cardinal Richard Cush-

John F. Kennedy, Jr. salutes his slain father.

ing of Boston spoke in English: "May the angels, dear Jack, lead you into paradise. May the martyrs receive you at your coming. May the spirit of God embrace you, and mayest thou, with all those who made the supreme sacrifice of dying for others, receive eternal rest and peace."[11]

After the service the coffin was placed back on the caisson for its trip to Arlington National Cemetery. The Marine Band played "Hail to the Chief," and President Kennedy's young son, John-John, on the day of his third birthday, saluted his dead father. Then the slow procession began again. This time the Kennedy family and other dignitaries rode in black limousines instead of walking the seven-mile route. Thousands of people watched them pass, and nearly everybody was sobbing. "You could see it in their faces, all along the way," said Kennedy aide Dave Powers. "Some of them had a frightened look, like, what are we going to do now? . . . It was the saddest thing you ever saw. Some of them were sadder, they told me later in letters, than if a relative had died."[12] Television viewers were crying, too.

At the cemetery the Marine Band played "The Star-Spangled Banner," and a Scottish bagpipe group, the Black Watch, piped "Mist-Covered Mountain." Just as the body was brought to the grave, a formation of 50 jets flew in a V overhead, with the last plane missing to symbolize Kennedy's death. Then *Air Force One* flew by and dipped its wings as a tribute to its lost president. A group of Irish cadets drilled silently. Prayers were said, and a 21-gun salute was fired followed by three rifle shots. A bugler played taps, and the flag was removed from the coffin and given to Mrs. Kennedy, who then lit the eternal flame.

Texas Senator Ralph Yarborough summed up the feelings of many on that day: "I was thinking of Kennedy and the loss to the world. It's an unspeakable tragedy for any president to be assassinated. Aside from [the Kennedy] family, it was a loss to the whole world. He was a hero to the whole world. People cried in every nation when he died."[13]

Once the funeral was over, Jackie Kennedy went back to the White House, where more than 200 representatives from 100 nations gathered to pay her their respects. Close friends and family members were there, too, and for a short time they slipped away from the rest of the mourners to hold a private birthday party for John-John, who was too young to understand the sadness happening all around him.

On the same day, in another part of the country, two other funerals were taking place. In Dallas, Officer John Tippit was laid to rest at Laurel Land Memorial Park, in a special section of the cemetery for people who had given their lives in community service. More than 5,000 people, including more than 700 police officers, attended his funeral, and it also was shown on television. His widow received a great deal of sympathy and support.

Meanwhile, in Fort Worth, Lee Harvey Oswald was being buried under quite different circumstances. Although Oswald's family had wanted a big funeral, the Secret Service arranged for a small, quiet burial at Rose Hill Cemetery. The only people present to mourn Oswald were his half brother, Robert, his mother, Marguerite, his wife, Marina, and his two little girls. Several reporters showed up, but because of a misunderstanding no minister came to perform the service. Dr. Louis Saunders, executive secretary of the Fort Worth Area Council of Churches, finally agreed to say a few words. When he was finished, he realized that no one had agreed to be a pallbearer. He asked a few reporters to carry the coffin from the chapel to the gravesite.

"There was a dim awareness in me," said Saunders later, "of the tremendous contrast between the beautiful and carefully worked-out service for President Kennedy and the very humble and stark service we were having [for Oswald]. . . . The service itself probably took about ten minutes. The family left very quickly after it was over."[14] One of the reporters who helped carry Oswald's coffin recalled, "I can assure you I had no sense of history that day. It was a story and an unpleasant story at the scene of a very unpleasant news day."[15]

Once Kennedy and Oswald had been laid to rest, the nation's grief turned to anger. Many people blamed the city of Dallas for the president's death. Police officers there got hateful phone calls from all over the world criticizing them for failing to protect the president. Dallas officials in turn

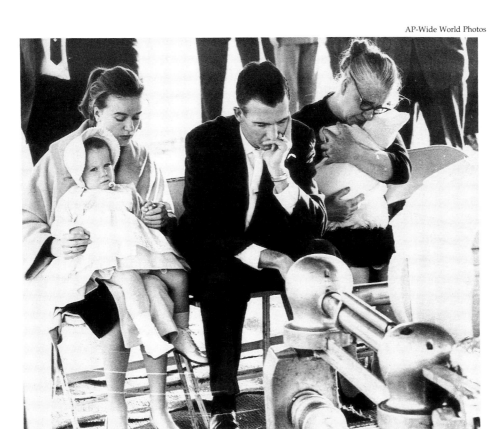

Marina Oswald and her two children attend the simple funeral of Lee Harvey Oswald, along with his half brother, Robert, and his mother, Marguerite.

blamed the FBI for the assassination. They pointed out that Agent Hosty and others knew about Oswald's Communist activities but didn't keep him away from the president's motorcade route. They also insisted that what had happened in Dallas could have happened anywhere.[16]

Others disagreed with this. Judge Sarah Hughes, who had sworn in President Johnson on *Air Force One*, stated publicly, "It could have happened anywhere, but Dallas, I'm sorry to say, has been conditioned by many people who have hate in their hearts and who seem to want to destroy."[17] This hatred was still evident after the assassination. Several Dallas residents who criticized the city in letters and articles that appeared in national magazines lost their jobs or were forced to leave town. Pastor

William A. Holmes received anonymous death threats after he appeared on the "CBS Evening News" and said, "There is no city in the United States which in recent months and years has been more acquiescent toward its extremists than Dallas."[18]

The city was also blamed for not protecting Oswald. An editorial in the *New York Times* stated, "The Dallas authorities, abetted and encouraged by the newspaper, TV and radio press, trampled on every principle of justice in their handling of Lee H. Oswald."[19] Many people suspected that the police had somehow helped Ruby to kill Oswald, and rumors began to grow about a conspiracy between Oswald and others who might have wanted the president dead.[20] The public demanded that something be done to discover the truth.

"With that single shot," wrote President Lyndon Johnson in his memoirs, "the outrage of a nation turned to skepticism and doubt. The atmosphere was poisonous and had to be cleared."[21]

On November 25 the Texas attorney general announced that a state court of inquiry would be held to investigate the assassination. Several senators immediately proposed that the Senate Judiciary Committee conduct its own investigation. One congressman suggested that a joint committee, composed of seven senators and seven representatives, handle the inquiry into the assassination.

Before any of these things could happen, President Lyndon Johnson decided "to avoid parallel investigations and to concentrate fact-finding in a body having the broadest national mandate."[22] On November 29 he signed an Executive Order creating a special commission, known as the Warren Commission, to investigate the assassination. Its job was to determine whether Lee Harvey Oswald really had killed President Kennedy, and if so, whether he had acted alone or as part of a conspiracy. President Johnson hoped that by creating the Warren Commission, he would put the issue to rest, but his actions only added to a controversy that has lasted for decades.

Chapter 6

THE CONTROVERSY BEGINS

T he Warren Commission was named for its chairman, Earl Warren, who was chief justice of the U.S. Supreme Court. Its six other members were two senators, Democrat Richard B. Russell and Republican John Sherman Cooper; two members of the House of Representatives, Democrat Hale Boggs and Republican Gerald R. Ford; and two attorneys, Allen W. Dulles, whom President Kennedy had fired as director of the CIA, and John J. McCloy, the assistant secretary of war during World War II.

On December 13 Congress granted these men the ability to call any witnesses and view any evidence they deemed necessary. The Warren Commission immediately began to assemble a staff and prepare for its investigation. The commission studied Secret Service and FBI reports on the assassination, a Department of State report on Oswald's attempted defection to the Soviet Union, and Dallas police reports on the deaths of Kennedy and Oswald.

The Warren Commission asked the FBI and Secret Service to begin questioning witnesses. The FBI conducted approximately 25,000 interviews; the Secret Service, 1,550. The Warren Commission started hearing witness testimony on February 3, 1964, although not all commissioners were pre-

Members of the Warren Commission. Chief Justice Earl Warren is fourth from the left.

sent at each session. A total of 94 witnesses appeared, with an additional 395 witnesses testifying before members of the Warren Commission's staff and 24 submitting sworn affidavits, or statements.

On September 24, 1964, after ten months of investigation, the Warren Commission submitted its 888-page report to President Johnson. Called *The Warren Report*, it was released to the general public on September 28. The Warren Commission published an additional 26 volumes ten weeks later; these held the evidence and testimony upon which *The Warren Report* was based. Neither *The Warren Report* nor its supporting volumes had an index until 1966, when author Sylvia Meagher published her *Subject Index to the Warren Report and Hearings and Exhibits.*

The Warren Report clearly stated the Warren Commission's findings: Only three shots had been fired at President Kennedy and Governor Connally, all of them from the sixth floor of the Texas School Book Depository; Oswald killed both the president and Officer Tippit; Jack Ruby had never known either Tippit or Oswald; and no one in the Dallas Police Department had helped Ruby kill Oswald. *The Warren Report* also said that even though Jack Ruby had many friends who were involved in organized crime, there was no proof that he himself was a criminal or had killed Oswald on the orders of anyone else.

The Warren Commission recommended that Congress immediately make it a federal crime for someone to assassinate the president or vice president of the United States. The Warren Commission further recommended that a president always have his personal physician nearby in case of emergency.

After publishing its conclusions, the Warren Commission put all of its evidence and investigative reports, which included countless statements made "off the record," in a special vault at the National Archives building. President Johnson ordered the vault sealed for 75 years. The public would not be allowed to see this material until the year 2039, when everyone involved with the assassination and its investigation would be dead.

The Warren Commission then dissolved itself, hoping it had put the matter to rest. But not everybody was willing to accept *The Warren Report* as fact. One of its strongest critics was attorney Mark Lane. Marguerite Oswald had hired Lane to represent her dead son's interests before the Warren Commission, but the commissioners refused to allow him to do so.

In 1966 Lane published *Rush to Judgment*, one of the first books to criticize the report. It was an instant best-seller. That same year Cornell University student Edward Jay Epstein, who had studied the Warren Commission as part of his Master's thesis in government, published *Inquest: The Warren Commission and the Establishment of Truth*. It, too, was highly critical of the Warren Commission's findings, as were *Whitewash— The Report on the Warren Report*, by retired journalist Harold Weisberg, and numerous magazine articles.

The main attack on the Warren Commission was that it had ignored anyone who did not say what it wanted to hear. This was particularly true with those witnesses who said gunshots had come from the grassy knoll. One woman, Jean Hill, insisted that she saw a man fire from behind a wooden fence at the top of the knoll. Hill later said that Arlen Specter, the attorney interviewing her for the Warren Commission, tried to get her to change her testimony.[1] Another witness, Julia Ann Mercer, had told Dallas police she saw a man with a rifle case near the knoll just before the assassination, but the Warren Commission never even questioned her.[2] Other people who reported seeing gunfire or smelling gunpowder at the knoll were also not asked to testify.[3]

Instead the Warren Commission relied upon an autopsy report from Bethesda Naval Hospital, which said that the president's wounds proved he had been shot from the rear. However, doctors at Parkland Hospital who had seen the president's body insisted he had been shot from the front.[4] Others noted that the Bethesda autopsy had been conducted improperly and that the report contained several obvious errors.[5]

Additional evidence that the president might have been shot from the front came from a man named Abraham Zapruder. At the exact moment of the shooting, Zapruder had been filming the president with an 8-millimeter movie camera equipped with a zoom lens. After the assassination he sold his film to *Life* magazine. *Life* made still prints from it and published them, but allowed only members of the Warren Commission to view the movie.

The Zapruder film clearly showed the president's head snapping backward at the moment of the fatal shot. It seemed as though this happened because he was shot from the front. However, the Warren Commission decided this movement was a reflex action that happened after the bullet had already hit the president from behind.[6]

The Zapruder film caused another problem for the Warren Commission. It showed that within six seconds, first the president was shot, next the governor was wounded, and then the president was struck again. Governor Connally said he thought he had been hit by a second bullet. However, after studying the timing of the film, the Warren Commission became certain that Oswald's rifle could not have fired two shots that close

Stills from the film taken by Abraham Zapruder show Jackie climbing over the back of the car to help a Secret Service agent aboard. The film was used by both the Warren Commission and Jim Garrison to support their claims.

together. Attorney Arlen Specter suggested that perhaps the first bullet had wounded both men.

"The Commission was thus confronted with a dilemma," wrote Epstein. "If it disregarded the evidence that Connally could not have been hit by the same bullet that hit Kennedy, and if it concluded that both men were hit by the same bullet, the credibility of the entire Report might be jeopardized. If, however, the Warren Commission concluded that both men were hit by separate bullets, the single-assassin theory would be untenable in terms of the established evidence and assumptions."[7] The commissioners argued a great deal over the "single-bullet theory," but in the end they stated that there was "very persuasive evidence from the experts to indicate that the same bullet that pierced the President's throat also caused Governor Connally's wounds."[8]

According to the Warren Commission, the first bullet hit the president in his upper back and came out through his throat. It then went into the governor's back, came out his chest, passed through his wrist, and ended up in his thigh. The Zapruder film clearly showed Governor Connally still sitting calmly well after the president was wounded, but the Warren Commission decided this only meant the governor had not reacted right away to his own injuries.[9]

Epstein, Lane, and many other *Warren Report* critics insisted that one bullet, which they called "magic," could not have injured both men.[10] They used line drawings of the bullet's path, or trajectory, to show that it would have had to change direction more than once to pass through the president and cause all of Governor Connally's wounds. However, these drawings ignored any movements the two men might have made during the shooting. Supporters of *The Warren Report* said that the way the president and the governor were positioned in the car, one in front of the other, made the single-bullet theory possible.

Another part of the argument over the single-bullet theory had to do with the condition of the bullet itself. While Governor Connally was at Parkland Hospital, someone found a bullet on his stretcher that the Warren Commission said was the "magic bullet." However, it barely looked as though it had been fired. Some experts said it could not have struck the governor's rib and shattered his wrist without being damaged.

In addition to the bullet from Parkland Hospital, two bullet fragments had been found in the front seat of the president's limousine. Experts felt that these fragments equaled one bullet, and investigators suggested that another bullet might have missed the car entirely. The Warren Commission was satisfied that these three bullets were the only shots fired, because three bullet shells had been discovered on the sixth floor of the Depository. However, many of the witnesses to the assassination were absolutely positive they had heard more than three shots. Some people said that at least one bullet had hit the pavement, and others believed that the president's body held additional bullet fragments.

The critics of *The Warren Report* succeeded in casting doubt on Oswald's guilt. According to a 1964 Harris poll, most Americans felt that Oswald had not acted alone. Some people wondered whether he had done any of the shooting at all. When Oswald left the marines, his marksmanship scores were poor, and only an expert rifleman could have hit the president from the sixth-floor window. Although he may have been practicing for the assassination, there was no evidence of it. Besides that, a Mannlicher-Carcano rifle was not a very accurate weapon.

There was also much debate over whether this gun was actually the one found at the Depository. One of the officers who was there said the rifle was a German 7.65 Mauser. Several other policemen who saw the gun also described it as a Mauser. Even the Dallas district attorney told reporters it was a Mauser. According to the Warren Commission, these were all just careless errors.[11] But a Mauser, which is highly accurate, would have been a good assassin's weapon.

Even if the Mannlicher-Carcano rifle really was the weapon found at the Depository, many people thought Oswald could not have shot the president and made it all the way down from the sixth floor to the second floor so quickly without being out of breath. According to the Warren Commission, during reenactments of the assassination someone was able to do so. However, Epstein, Lane, and others pointed out that none of the

Warren Commission's expert marksmen was ever able to duplicate the shots that hit the president and Governor Connally.

Critics also doubted whether Oswald killed Officer Tippit. They did not believe the statements in *The Warren Report* about Oswald's movements after the assassination. The Warren Commission used timed reenactments to show that it was possible for Oswald to get to the site of Tippit's murder using the bus and cab, but did not allow for any delays because of traffic or other difficulties. Not only that, but several witnesses to Tippit's shooting were unable to identify Oswald in a lineup, and their testimony contained many contradictions.

More than one kind of bullet was found in the officer's body, which meant either that the killer had handloaded different types of ammunition into his gun or that there was more than one killer. One witness, Acquilla Clemons, told police that she had seen a second man standing near Tippit's patrol car just moments before he was shot, but the Warren Commission never questioned her. Instead they relied upon the statements of a woman named Helen Markham.

Markham told the Warren Commission that there had been only one gunman. She said she had first noticed him walking along the street, then saw Tippit's patrol car approach the man slowly from the rear and stop alongside of him. Markham was certain that Tippit had leaned out of his patrol car window to talk to the man before getting out of his car and being shot. However, other witnesses at the scene were equally certain that the window of Tippit's car had been rolled up, and they said that Markham had arrived on the scene only *after* the shooting had taken place. Even Assistant Counsel Joseph A. Ball, who helped to conduct the Warren Commission's investigation, called Helen Markham an unreliable witness.[12]

"Friendly witnesses gave testimony without fear of criticism or cross-examination," wrote Lane. "[They] were led through their paces by lawyers who . . . asked leading questions, while those few who challenged the Government's case were often harassed. . . . Important witnesses with invaluable evidence to give were never called."[13]

The Warren Commission completely ignored witnesses who said that

Jack Ruby knew most of the Dallas police force and that police allowed Ruby to break certain liquor laws in return for free drinks at his clubs. "[There is] no credible evidence that Ruby sought special favors from police officers or attempted to bribe them," *The Warren Report* stated. And although more than one person said that Ruby had known Officer Tippit, who was shot only two blocks from Ruby's home, the Warren Commission concluded that the two men had never met.[14]

Ruby appeared before two members of the Warren Commission, Chief Justice Earl Warren and Congressman Gerald R. Ford, on June 7, 1964, more than six months after the assassination. By that time Ruby had already been tried and found guilty of murdering Oswald, so the questioning was conducted at the Dallas County Jail in the presence of the sheriff of Dallas, the attorney general of Texas, and the Dallas district attorney.

When the commissioners began interviewing Ruby, he immediately made it plain that he would not talk unless he was taken out of the Dallas jail. He asked the Chief Justice again and again to get him to Washington so that he could testify without fear. Warren refused his request, even though Ruby insisted his life was in danger, and Ruby never did tell the commissioners what he knew.

Three years later he was dead. By this time his murder conviction had been overturned by the Texas Court of Appeals on technical grounds. While awaiting a retrial, he caught a cold and was sent to the Dallas sheriff's office for treatment. According to police, his cold worsened and he was sent to a hospital, where he was found to have cancer. Ruby died in January 1967.

That same year New Orleans District Attorney Jim Garrison opened his own investigation into the assassination. Long before *The Warren Report* was published, Garrison had given the FBI information about Oswald's three months in New Orleans. During that time, Oswald had been seen with David Ferrie, a man known for his anti-Castro activities. Ferrie had also been a pilot for the CIA at the time of the Bay of Pigs incident. When Garrison read the full 26 volumes of the Warren Commission's findings, he was dissatisfied with the way the case had been handled.[15]

From the beginning, Garrison suspected that Oswald had been some kind of government agent. He knew it was unusual for an ordinary marine to be given lessons in the Russian language. He also knew that Oswald's mother said her son had worked for the U.S. government. In the course of his two-year investigation, Garrison uncovered evidence that Oswald had spent time not only with Ferrie but also with former FBI agent Guy Banister, whom he believed did some work related to Cuba for the CIA.

Garrison also believed that Oswald knew Clay Shaw. Shaw was the director of the International Trade Mart in New Orleans, but Garrison believed that Shaw also worked for the CIA. A friend of Ferrie's said that Ferrie and Shaw, with Oswald present, had discussed a plot to kill the president and blame it on Castro. Garrison decided to prosecute Shaw for the assassination.

The case went to trial in 1969. By that time both Banister and Ferrie were dead, and the federal government refused to cooperate with Garrison's case. The press made fun of him, and he knew he had little chance of winning.

Garrison's first task was to convince the jury that at least one of the shots fired during the assassination had come from the grassy knoll. To do this, he subpoenaed the Zapruder film from *Life* magazine and showed it in open court. This was the first time the film was ever viewed openly, and it had a powerful effect. Later, many of the jurors would say that Garrison had proved there was more than one assassin.

New Orleans District Attorney Jim Garrison speaks to reporters about his reopening of the investigation into the Kennedy assassination.

AP–Wide World Photos

However, they did not believe that Clay Shaw had been involved in a plot to kill the president. In the end, they found him not guilty.

When Garrison lost his case, members of the news media said it was because *The Warren Report* was right. Still, some people would not accept this. Over the next few years, they began to demand a new investigation into the assassination. Then, in 1975, the Zapruder film was finally shown on national television, and the pressure to reopen the case increased.

At that time Congress had been working to strengthen the Freedom of Information Act (FOIA). Originally enacted in 1966 and amended in 1974 and 1976, the FOIA requires all agencies of the federal government to turn over any nonclassified information, with a few exceptions, to anyone making a reasonable request. Using the FOIA, Mark Lane and others obtained thousands of documents related to the Kennedy assassination that only added to the controversy.

Finally, in fall 1976, the U.S. House of Representatives created the House Select Committee on Assassinations. This was not only a response to critics of the Warren Commission but also a reaction to a Senate investigation earlier that year on government intelligence activities. The Senate investigation had revealed that in the early 1960s the CIA had used members of organized crime in an effort to assassinate Castro, and Congress became worried about how this might relate to the Kennedy assassination.

In March 1977 Louis Stokes, a Democratic congressman from Ohio, was named head of the House Select Committee on Assassinations, which had a total of 12 members. The House Select Committee's main job was to determine who had assassinated President Kennedy and Martin Luther King, Jr., the slain civil rights leader. The House Select Committee's members were also to decide whether the government had done all it could to protect these men's lives and investigate their deaths.

The House Select Committee spent 30 months and $5.5 million hearing 335 witnesses, conducting more than 4,924 interviews, and examining countless documents. Much of their work was done in private, but in 1978 they held 35 days of public hearings on the evidence and 2 days openly discussing government policy regarding assassination.

The House Select Committee published its findings in January 1979 as a one-volume summary report released to the general public. It also made available its hearing testimony and other reports in a 27-volume work. According to the House Select Committee, most of the Warren Commission's conclusions were correct. All of the bullets that struck President Kennedy and Governor Connally had come from the Texas School Book Depository, and one of them had passed through both men. The Mannlicher-Carcano rifle was the gun found at the Depository, it was the assassin's weapon, and it had belonged to Oswald.

However, the House Select Committee also said it was highly probable that someone had fired at the president from the grassy knoll. It based this conclusion on more than just witness testimony. Using tape recordings of the sounds of the assassination made by the Dallas police, acoustical experts were able to tell that one of the shots had indeed come from the knoll. The House Select Committee believed this bullet must have missed the car, because the autopsy report from Bethesda Naval Hospital said the president had only been hit from behind.

Since there was a second gunman, the House Select Committee had to conclude there *had been* a conspiracy to kill the president. As to who took part in that conspiracy, the House Select Committee said it was not the Soviet government, the Cuban government, organized crime, the Secret Service, the FBI, or the CIA. It did think that individual members of an anti-Castro Cuban group could have been involved. It specifically mentioned Oswald's acquaintance with David Ferrie and Guy Banister, just as District Attorney Jim Garrison had several years earlier, but it did not conclude they had worked for the U.S. government.

The House Select Committee also suspected a man named Carlos Marcello, a leader of organized crime based in New Orleans. Marcello knew Ferrie, and also quite possibly both Oswald and Ruby. Another crime boss, Santos Trafficante, also had connections to Ruby and could have been involved. Trafficante had participated in the Mafia and CIA attempts to have Castro assassinated.

In addition, the House Select Committee concluded that the Warren

Commission should have examined Jack Ruby more carefully. He might have been involved in the assassination, and it was likely that he had planned in advance to shoot Oswald with the help of someone in the Dallas Police Department. The House Select Committee criticized the way the Warren Commission handled this and other parts of its investigation. It said the Dallas police, the Secret Service, the FBI, the CIA, and the Department of Justice had all made serious errors in judgment. However, it added that these groups had been acting "in good faith."[16]

The House Select Committee did not discover who exactly was behind the conspiracy. Its members said that was the job of the Justice Department, and suggested that more investigation was necessary. Many Americans agreed with this.

In the years since the House Select Committee's report, interest in the Kennedy assassination has grown. More and more books have been written about who might have killed President Kennedy and why. Their authors include legal, technical, and political experts, as well as former District Attorney Jim Garrison, who wrote about the Clay Shaw trial.

In 1991 movie director Oliver Stone used Garrison's book, *On the Trail of the Assassins*, and other sources to create his movie *JFK*. Viewed by millions of people, *JFK* proposed that Kennedy was killed by a conspiracy involving members of the CIA, FBI, and perhaps even the highest levels of government and the military. According to Stone, the president was planning to withdraw American troops from Vietnam, and he was assassinated by people who wanted U.S. involvement in the war there to continue.[17]

Even before *JFK* was released, it created controversy. Some people believed its theories, while others opposed them. In any case, most Americans, including members of government, began to question why the files on the Kennedy assassination had to remain sealed until the year 2039. Some files were opened in 1993, and efforts are now under way to have the remaining ones opened sooner, in the hopes that the public might at last discover the truth about President Kennedy's death.

Chapter 7

THE LEGACY OF JFK

Although his time in office was brief, President Kennedy left much behind for us to remember him by. He had a clear vision of what he wanted for America, and out of that vision came many social programs that are still with us today.

One of the best known is the Peace Corps, established by the president in 1961. Its purpose is to offer help to the poorer countries of the world, and its members are volunteers of all races and religions. After a difficult training program, the men and women of the Corps spend two years or more in remote villages, where they build roads, try to improve living conditions, and teach people how to read, write, farm, and keep themselves healthy. From the moment it was created, the Peace Corps has attracted thousands upon thousands of dedicated Americans willing to give their time and care to people in need.

President Kennedy recognized the value of this kind of public service. "Ask not what your country can do for you," he said in his inaugural address. "Ask what you can do for your country."[1] He wanted people to understand that their participation in government and its programs was important. He felt that the United States was facing a "New Frontier," a time of new challenges and new opportunities, and he used this phrase to describe a group of policies he hoped would improve the quality of life in America.

John F. Kennedy Library

Kennedy greets Peace Corps volunteers during a ceremony at the White House to mark the launch of the service organization he founded.

An important part of the New Frontier was civil rights. At the time President Kennedy took office, African-Americans were often kept from participating in state elections because of laws that said voters had to be able to read well or own land. They also were not allowed to eat in the same restaurants, sleep in the same hotels, use the same rest rooms, or attend the same schools as everybody else, even though the United States Supreme Court had ruled against segregation in several recent cases. Some state governments, particularly in the South, refused to abide by the decisions of the Court, and continued to discriminate against African-Americans, whom, in charitable moments, they called "coloreds."

In response, African-Americans began demonstrating against segregation. One of the most important protests was the Freedom Ride, organized by the Congress of Racial Equality right after the U.S. Supreme Court ruled that bus terminals and their lunch counters could not be segregated. The Freedom Ride began in May 1961 when two buses filled with both whites and African-Americans began a trip from Washington, D.C., into the deep South. Their purpose was to stop at various bus terminals to test the new ruling.

President Kennedy meets with Dr. Martin Luther King, Jr. and other civil rights leaders.

When the Freedom Riders reached Atlanta, Georgia, they picked up Dr. Martin Luther King, Jr., a leader of the civil rights movement. With King they traveled into Alabama, where angry mobs beat them with pipes and clubs. These acts of violence were reported around the world.

President Kennedy ordered protection for the Freedom Riders and spoke out against their attackers. In September 1961 he asked the Interstate Commerce Commission to issue new regulations making it illegal to segregate in interstate bus terminals. Later, he ordered the Justice Department to enforce all existing civil rights laws, and he tried to create a new law that would strengthen voting rights; end racial discrimination in hotels, restaurants, and similar places; desegregate the public schools; and allow the federal government to withhold money from states that did not treat all people equally. Although Kennedy's Civil Rights Act was not passed until after his death, it was one of the most significant pieces of legislation from his administration.

Another law passed immediately after Kennedy's assassination was his Higher Education Act, which provided funds for the building of community colleges, graduate schools, and libraries. Kennedy was committed to improving education, and during his presidency he worked for several laws that aided schools and students. He spoke often about the need for the federal government to provide money for the public schools and to improve teacher training programs.

Other issues that were part of Kennedy's New Frontier included job training for the unemployed, higher wages for employees, and better working conditions across the country. Kennedy was particularly worried about people in the inner cities and depressed rural areas who wanted to work but could find no jobs. In 1961 he signed the Area Redevelopment Act (ARA), which provided government loans to attract new businesses to places of high unemployment. ARA also funded job retraining for those who would work in these new businesses, as well as grants to the poorest of communities.

Kennedy was equally concerned with the problems of the elderly, who he felt needed better medical care. Throughout his presidency he tried to create Medicare, a type of health insurance for people over 65. However, just as with his Civil Rights Act and education bills, Congress approved Medicare only after Kennedy's death. This was partly because President Johnson took advantage of public sympathy to push his predecessor's bills through a once reluctant Congress.[2]

President Johnson also managed to convince Congress to approve a massive tax cut originally proposed by Kennedy. The cut stimulated the economy and created a period of prosperity for the country. In addition, Kennedy's program reformed the way taxes were calculated in the United States, winning praise from economic experts.

Another of Kennedy's programs involved space exploration. In his State of the Union address to Congress in May 1961, President Kennedy said, "I believe this nation should commit itself to achieving the goal, before this decade is out, of landing a man on the Moon and returning him safely to Earth."[3] At that time, the Russians had already launched the first manned orbital flight, and their space program far surpassed the one in the United States. Kennedy's call for action changed all that. Soon the United States was moving to the forefront in space technology.

On February 20, 1962, Major John H. Glenn orbited the earth three times in his Mercury space capsule, *Friendship 7*. Then, between May 1962 and May 1963, there were three more Mercury missions. Lieutenant Commander M. Scott Carpenter orbited the earth 3 times, Commander Walter M. Schirra 6 times, and Air Force Major L. Gordon Cooper 22 times. By the time of President Kennedy's death, the United States had showed its commitment to further space exploration, and the entire launching area in Florida, which included Cape Canaveral and Merritt Island, was renamed the John F. Kennedy Space Center. Cape Canaveral was called Cape Kennedy from 1963 to 1973.

Even though President Kennedy encouraged American scientists to compete against the Soviets in the race for space, he also envisioned a time when the people of both countries would work together. During his inaugural speech, he talked at length about "the quest for peace" and called for the United States and the Soviet Union to stop creating nuclear weapons. President Kennedy wanted arms control, and on September 25, 1961, he went before the United Nations to talk about the need for disarmament. The next day he signed a bill establishing the United States Arms Control and Disarmament Agency.

In June of the following year, President Kennedy gave a speech in which he said he wanted "genuine peace, the kind of peace that makes life on earth worth living, the kind that enables men and nations to grow and to hope and to build a better life for their children—not merely peace for Americans but peace for all men and women—not merely peace in our time but peace for all time." He spoke about the need for the people of the world to get along, because "in the final analysis, our most basic common link is that we all inhabit this small planet. We all breathe the same air. We all cherish our children's future. And we are all mortal."[4]

This speech encouraged the Soviet Union to reexamine its attitudes toward the United States and nuclear war. On June 20 it helped to create a direct telephone connection between Moscow and Washington, D.C., a "hot line" that allowed the leaders of both countries to speak to each other on a moment's notice. After that, officials from the United States, Soviet

Union, and Great Britain met to discuss placing limits on the testing of nuclear weapons. This led to a treaty that banned nuclear tests in outer space, the earth's atmosphere, and the oceans of the world. President Kennedy called this treaty "an important first step—a step towards peace—a step towards reason—a step away from war."[5]

President Kennedy wanted people to live together in harmony. Improved U.S.-Soviet relations, the Peace Corps, and the Civil Rights Act were all just a part of his goals for the country and the world. Had he lived to finish his first term in office, had he gone on to serve a second term, no one knows what he might have accomplished. He was a dynamic man who always acted on his beliefs and tried to do what he thought was right.

In a foreword to a memorial edition of Kennedy's book *Profiles in Courage*, his brother Robert wrote of him that "his life had an import, meant something to the country while he was alive. More significant, however, is what we do with what is left, with what has been started."[6] Robert Kennedy knew that it was important for the things his brother stood for to continue.

Although President Kennedy rests in Arlington National Cemetery, his words still inspire us to greatness. At his grave the eternal flame burns forever as a testament to the permanence of all he left behind. "Let the word go forth from this time and place," Kennedy said at his inauguration, "to friend and foe alike, that the torch has been passed to a new generation of Americans . . . unwilling to witness or permit the slow undoing of those human rights to which this nation has always been committed, and to which we are committed today at home and around the world."[7]

Many people will never forget what President Kennedy stood for. "You can recall those years of grace, that time of hope," his brother Edward once said. "The spark still glows. The journey never ends. The dream shall never die."[8] President Kennedy is remembered for his great accomplishments, not just because he was assassinated. "The courage of life is often a less dramatic spectacle than the courage of a final moment," President Kennedy wrote in *Profiles in Courage*, "but it is no less a magnificent mixture of triumph and tragedy."[9]

NOTES

Chapter 1

1. Thomas C. Reeves, *A Question of Character* (Rocklin, Cal.: Prima, 1992), p. 34.
2. Ralph G. Martin, *A Hero for Our Time* (New York: Ballantine Books, 1983), p. 25.
3. Martin, p. 39.
4. Ibid, p. 40.
5. Ibid.
6. John H. Davis, *The Kennedys: Dynasty and Disaster* (New York: Shapolsky, 1992), p. 132.
7. Martin, p. 44.
8. Reeves, p. 98.
9. Ibid, p. 104.
10. John F. Kennedy, *Profiles in Courage— Commemorative Edition* (New York: Harper & Row, 1964), p. 1.
11. Reeves, p. 201.
12. Ibid, p. 213.
13. Martin, p. 309.
14. Reeves, p. 378.
15. Ibid.
16. Ibid, p. 392.
17. Martin, p. 470.
18. Ibid.
19. Ibid, p. 465.
20. Reeves, p. 411.
21. Martin, p. 465.
22. Davis, p. 423.
23. Ibid, p. 362.
24. Martin, p. 500.
25. Ibid, p. 503.
26. Jim Bishop, *The Day Kennedy Was Shot* (New York: Funk & Wagnalls, 1968), p. 70.
27. Martin, p. 515.

Chapter 2

1. Bishop, pp. 24–25.
2. Ibid, p. 26.
3. Ibid, p. 124.
4. The *Dallas Morning News*, November 22: The Day Remembered as Reported by The *Dallas Morning News* (Dallas: Taylor, 1990), p. 17.
5. Ibid.
6. Davis, p. 523.
7. The *Dallas Morning News*, p. 18; Bishop, pp. 174-175.
8. The *Dallas Morning News*, p. 18.
9. Ibid, pp. 21–22.
10. Ibid, p. 20.
11. Ibid, p. 26.
12. Bishop, pp. 211–214.
13. The *Dallas Morning News*, p. 22.
14. Ibid, pp. 26–27.
15. Ibid, pp. 35–36.
16. Ibid, p. 39.
17. Bishop, p. 283.
18. Ibid, p. 288.
19. Ibid, p. 289.
20. Martin, p. 520.
21. The *Dallas Morning News*, p. 42.
22. Bishop, p. 316.
23. The *Dallas Morning News*, p. 42.
24. Bishop, pp. 355–356.
25. Ibid, pp. 412–413.
26. Martin, p. 522.
27. The *Dallas Morning News*, p. 153.
28. Arthur M. Schlesinger, Jr., *A Thousand Days: John F. Kennedy in the White House* (Boston: Houghton Mifflin, 1965), p. 1029.
29. Howard Roffman, *Presumed Guilty: Lee Harvey Oswald in the Assassination of President Kennedy* (Cranberry, New Jersey: Associated University Presses, 1975), p. 76.

Chapter 3

1. The President's Commission on the Assassination of President John F. Kennedy, *The Warren Report: The Report of the President's Commission on the Assassination of President John F. Kennedy* (Washington, D. C.: Associated Press, 1964), p. 29.
2. Ibid, p. 57.
3. Bishop, p. 183.
4. *The Warren Report*, p. 62.

5. Ibid, p. 66; Bishop, pp. 233–235.
6. Bishop, pp. 250–251.
7. *The Warren Report*, pp. 62–63.
8. Mark Lane, *Rush to Judgment* (New York: Holt, Rinehart & Winston, 1966), pp. 176–178, 197, 204–207; Bishop, pp. 255–259.
9. Bishop, p. 262.
10. Ibid, p. 274.
11. The *Dallas Morning News*, p. 31.
12. Bishop, p. 278.
13. The *Dallas Morning News*, p. 40.
14. Bishop, pp. 323–324.
15. *The Warren Report*, pp. 303–304.
16. Ibid, pp. 342–344.
17. Ibid, p. 84.

Chapter 4

1. Bishop, p. 301.
2. Ibid.
3. Ibid, p. 302.
4. The *Dallas Morning News*, p. 64; Bishop, p. 302.
5. Bishop, p. 302.
6. Bishop, pp. 303, 317; *The Warren Report*, p. 255.
7. Bishop, pp. 323–324; *The Warren Report*, pp. 253–254.
8. Lane, pp. 90–91.
9. Ibid, p. 281.
10. *The Warren Report*, p. 57.
11. Lane, pp. 100–104.
12. Ibid, pp. 100–108.
13. Ibid, p. 159; *The Warren Report*, pp. 59–66.
14. Lane, pp. 160–161, 169.
15. *The Warren Report*, p. 64.
16. Lane, p. 166.
17. Ibid, pp. 169–170, 200–203.
18. Ibid, p. 144.
19. Ibid, pp. 142–143.
20. *The Warren Report*, p. 73.
21. Lane, pp. 142–147; Roffman, pp. 56–58, 162–171.
22. *The Warren Report*, pp. 237–239, 248–250; Lane, pp. 114–120.
23. *The Warren Report*, pp. 34–35, 49–50, 250.
24. The *Dallas Morning News*, p. 65.
25. Bishop, pp. 12, 357–362, *The Warren Report*, pp. 50–51, 251–252; Lane, pp. 344–362.
26. The *Dallas Morning News*, p. 43; Bishop, p. 281.
27. Bishop, pp. 301–303, 317, 398–399, 455–456.
28. The *Dallas Morning News*, p. 65.
29. *The Warren Report*, p. 264.
30. Ibid, pp. 252, 264.
31. Ibid, p. 264.
32. Ibid, pp. 50–51, 250.
33. Jay David, ed., *The Weight of the Evidence* (New York: Meredith Press, 1968), pp. 176–181; Lane, pp. 260–272; Roffman, p. 146; United States House of Representatives, *The Final Assassinations Report: Report of the Select Committee on Assassinations* (New York: Bantam Books, 1979), pp. 193–194; Bill Sloan with Jean Hill, *JFK: The Last Dissenting Witness* (Gretna, Louisiana: Pelican, 1992), pp. 47, 103–107.
34. The *Dallas Morning News*, p. 54; David, p. 177.
35. Lane, pp. 229–240; Bishop, p. 349; *The Warren Report*, pp. 358–359.
36. *The Warren Report*, pp. 351–361; The *Dallas Morning News*, pp. 129–131; U. S. House, pp. 182–186.
37. The *Dallas Morning News*, p. 131; U. S. House of Representatives, p. 194; *The Warren Report*, pp. 283, 357–358.
38. David, pp. 176–179; *The Warren Report*, pp. 85–94.
39. *The Warren Report*, p. 85; Lane, p. 209; The *Dallas Morning News*, pp. 72–73.
40. The *Dallas Morning News*, p. 74.
41. Ibid.
42. Ibid; David, pp. 176–178; Lane, pp. 209–211.
43. *The Warren Report*, p. 85.
44. The *Dallas Morning News*, p. 82.
45. David, p. 177; The *Dallas Morning News*, p. 82; *The Warren Report*, pp. 85–86.
46. Lane, p. 211; *The Warren Report*, p. 87.
47. The *Dallas Morning News*, p. 75.
48. Ibid, pp. 75–77.

49. *The Warren Report*, p. 87; David, p. 177; The *Dallas Morning News*, pp. 81–82.

Chapter 5

1. The *Dallas Morning News*, p. 62.
2. Martin, p. 523.
3. The *Dallas Morning News*, pp. 62–63.
4. Ibid, p. 66.
5. Ibid, pp. 59–62.
6. Ibid, pp. 63–64.
7. Ibid, p. 88.
8. Ibid, p. 92.
9. Ibid.
10. Davis, p. 534.
11. Ibid, p. 535.
12. The *Dallas Morning News*, p. 107.
13. Ibid, p. 113.
14. Ibid, p. 116.
15. Ibid.
16. Ibid, pp. 144–150.
17. Schlesinger, p. 1027.
18. The *Dallas Morning News*, p. 146.
19. Ibid, p. 145; Roffman, p. 75.
20. David, pp. 3–9.
21. Davis, p. 555.
22. *The Warren Report*, p. vii.

Chapter 6

1. Edward Jay Epstein, *Inquest: The Warren Commission and the Establishment of Truth* (New York: Viking Press, 1966), p. 90; Lane, p. 41; Sloan, pp. 100–104; Jim Garrison, *On the Trail of the Assassins* (New York: Sheridan Square Press, 1988), pp. 15–21.
2. Lane, pp. 29–30.
3. Ibid, pp. 43–45; David S. Lifton, *Best Evidence: Disguise and Deception in the Assassination of John F. Kennedy* (New York: Macmillan, 1980), pp. 15–16; David, pp. 112–115; U. S. House of Representatives, p. 98.
4. Lifton, pp. 55–69.
5. Roffman, pp. 107–130; David, pp. 77–93; Lane, pp. 46–68; Lifton, pp. 308–337.

6. *The Warren Report*, pp. 40–47; Lane, pp. 69–80; Garrison, pp. xiii, 239.
7. Epstein, p. 148.
8. Ibid, p. 149.
9. *The Warren Report*, pp. 34–46; Lane, pp. 69–80.
10. Lane, pp. 69–80; David, pp. 58–93, 121–145; Lifton, pp. 338–379; Epstein, pp. 116–125; Garrison, pp. 240–241.
11. U. S. House of Representatives, pp. 44–46; Lane, pp. 114–120; *The Warren Report*, pp. 274–275.
12. Epstein, pp. 134–136.
13. Lane, p. 398.
14. Lane, pp. 248–259; *The Warren Report*, p. 284.
15. Garrison, pp. 3–11, 14–23; Mark Lane, *Plausible Denial: Was the CIA Involved in the Assassination of JFK?* (New York: Thunder's Mouth Press, 1991), pp. 221–225.
16. U. S. House of Representatives, pp. 329–330.
17. Oliver Stone. Introduction to *JFK: The CIA, Vietnam, and the Plot to Assassinate John F. Kennedy* by L. Fletcher Prouty (New York: Birch Lane Press, 1992).

Chapter 7

1. Reeves, p. 234.
2. John A. Garraty and Robert A. McCaughey, *The American Nation: A History of the United States since 1865*. Volume 2 (New York: Harper & Row, 1987), pp. 862–864.
3. Kenneth Gatland et al., *The Illustrated Encyclopedia of Space Technology: A Comprehensive History of Space Exploration* (New York: Harmony Books, 1981), p. 152.
4. Reeves, p. 398.
5. Ibid, p. 401.
6. Kennedy, p. xiii.
7. Reeves, p. 233.
8. Martin, p. 534.
9. Kennedy, p. 216.

FOR FURTHER READING

Bernstein, Irving. *Promises Kept: John F. Kennedy's New Frontier*. New York: Oxford University Press, 1991.

Bishop, Jim. *The Day Kennedy Was Shot*. New York: Funk & Wagnalls, 1968.

Brown, Walt. *The People v. Lee Harvey Oswald*. New York: Carroll & Graf, 1992.

The *Dallas Morning News*. November 22: The Day Remembered as Reported by The *Dallas Morning News*. Dallas: Taylor, 1990.

David, Jay, ed. *The Weight of the Evidence: The Warren Report and Its Critics*. New York: Meredith Press, 1968.

Davis, John H. *The Kennedys: Dynasty and Disaster*. New York: Shapolsky, 1992.

Donovan, Robert J. *PT 109: John F. Kennedy in World War II*. New York: McGraw-Hill, 1961.

Epstein, Edward Jay. *Inquest: The Warren Commission and the Establishment of Truth*. New York: Viking Press, 1966.

Garraty, John A., and Robert A. McCaughey. *The American Nation: A History of the United States since 1865*. Vol. 2. New York: Harper & Row, 1987.

Garrison, Jim. *On the Trail of the Assassins*. New York: Sheridan Square Press, 1988.

Gatland, Kenneth et al. *The Illustrated Encyclopedia of Space Technology: A Comprehensive History of Space Exploration*. New York: Harmony Books, 1981.

Kennedy, John F. *Profiles in Courage—Commemorative Edition*. New York: Harper & Row, 1964.

Lane, Mark. *Plausible Denial: Was the CIA Involved in the Assassination of JFK?* New York: Thunder's Mouth Press, 1991.

———. *Rush to Judgment*. New York: Holt, Rinehart & Winston, 1966.

Lifton, David S. *Best Evidence: Disguise and Deception in the Assassination of John F. Kennedy*. New York: Macmillan, 1980.

Manchester, William. *The Death of a President: November 1963*. New York: Harper & Row, 1967.

Martin, Ralph G. *A Hero for Our Time*. New York: Ballantine Books, 1983.

Mills, Judie. *John F. Kennedy*. New York: Franklin Watts, 1988.

The President's Commission on the Assassination of President John F. Kennedy. *The Warren Report: The Report of the President's Commission on the Assassination of President John F. Kennedy*. Washington, D.C.: Associated Press, 1964.

Prouty, L. Fletcher. *JFK: The CIA, Vietnam, and the Plot to Assassinate John F. Kennedy*, New York: Birch Lane Press, 1992.

Reeves, Thomas C. *A Question of Character*. Rocklin, CA: Prima, 1992.

Roffman, Howard. *Presumed Guilty: Lee Harvey Oswald in the Assassination of President Kennedy*. Cranberry, NJ: Associated University Presses, 1975.

Salinger, Pierre E. *With Kennedy*. Garden City, NY: Doubleday, 1966.

Schlesinger, Arthur M., Jr. *A Thousand Days: John F. Kennedy in the White House*. Boston: Houghton Mifflin, 1965.

Selfridge, John W. *John F. Kennedy: Courage in Crisis*. New York: Fawcett Columbine, 1989.

Sloan, Bill, with Jean Hill. *JFK: The Last Dissenting Witness*. Gretna, LA: Pelican, 1992.

United States House of Representatives. *The Final Assassinations Report: Report of the Select Committee on Assassinations*. New York: Bantam Books, 1979.

Weisberg, Harold. *Whitewash—The Report on the Warren Report*. New York: Dell, 1966.

INDEX